DWARF FRUIT TREES
FOR THE HOME GARDENER

DWARF
FRUIT TREES

for the
HOME GARDENER

by

LAWRENCE SOUTHWICK

GARDEN WAY PUBLISHING
CHARLOTTE, VERMONT 05445

Standard Book Number: (pbk) 0-88266-010-1 (cloth)
Library of Congress Catalog Card Number: 72-90892

Garden Way Publishing, Charlotte, Vermont 05445

Printed in the United States of America

"Trees full of soft foliage; blossoms fresh with spring beauty; and, finally,—fruit, rich, bloom-dusted, melting, and luscious—such are the treasures of the orchard and the garden, temptingly offered to every landholder in this bright and sunny, though temperate climate."

A. J. Downing (1845)

The author, Lawrence Southwick, began his dwarf fruit tree work at the University of Massachusetts, where he was a research horticulturist for many years. Two of his projects concerned the propagation and testing of improved dwarfing rootstocks and the management of dwarf fruit tree plantings.

Lawrence Southwick grew up on a diversified farm in central Massachusetts. He obtained a Bachelor of Science degree at the state university, specializing in fruit growing, general horticulture and agronomy. Later he earned the Master of Science degree and became a member of the faculty. He is the author of several experiment station bulletins and research papers and also has contributed to farm magazines.

After this experience, he transferred to a technical position with a leading manufacturer of agricultural chemicals in the Midwest, and continued in research and development work. His travels in this country and abroad have brought him to many fruit growing areas, including England and France, where many of the dwarfing rootstocks were developed. The author has telescoped extensive research and practical knowledge into this simplified readable guide for the backyard fruit grower.

Contents

1

Why Have Dwarf Trees?

A dwarf fruit tree, like a pigmy, grows old—but never grows up. Astonishingly, however, it bears full-sized fruit.

The modern dwarf has been developed after many decades of experiment and research. Lately it has attracted much interest. For the little trees bear early in life, and in amazing profusion. They are easy to plant, take little space, are simple to care for, yet in quality their fruit is equal to the best. They can at once be a fascinating hobby and make a substantial, economical contribution to the family larder. Without question they are one of the most successful developments of modern science for the home food grower.

You do not have to be an expert in horticulture to grow dwarf fruit trees. All you need is—first, a sincere, continuing interest in growing plants; second, a suitable soil and a small amount of sunny land.

A good gardener often makes a good fruit grower. The person who waxes enthusiastic in the invigorating springtime, but whose ambition wanes in the sultry days of summer, is hardly one to find a lasting fascination in dwarf fruit culture. It is to those folks who are genuinely interested in growing their own fruit supply economically, and to those who just naturally find a special esthetic exhilaration in fine-looking, full-flavored fruit grown through their own efforts, that dwarf fruit production is most appealing.

Red Spy apple on Malling IX rootstock in third year. A Spy on Standard Stock requires up to 9 or 10 years to come into bearing.

But perhaps you are saying to yourself: "If I'm going to plant some fruit trees, why not have big ones and get lots more fruit?" Such doubts are not likely to endure after we get down to details as to why dwarf trees are better suited for the home orchard.

Historical Background

If you are of the older generation you will remember that practically every town and country family used to grow many varieties of luscious fruit at home on standard trees. Much of the advance in American fruit culture may be traced to the important roles played by the amateur fruit growers of earlier days. Later, however, home fruit culture went into a decline. In fact, until recently there has been a feeling among horticulturists, and home growers too, that the raising of tree fruits—and apples in particular—should be limited to commercial growers because of the difficulties involved in producing "clean fruit." This is primarily because of the increased severity of the disease and insect problem. The main reasons for this trend seem to be:

(1) Conditions have been favorable for an increase in the insect population, because of better forage as a result of increased commercial plantings.

(2) Any insecticide program may kill beneficial and predatory insects as well as harmful ones. Predators normally kill many destructive insects.

(3) Insects develop immunity, or at least resistance, to poisons.

(4) New insects have been introduced and spread.

(5) Some popular varieties of fruit trees, such as McIntosh, for example, are more susceptible to disease attack than many of the older sorts.

My father and others have often remarked how much easier it was to grow fruit many years ago than it is today. Pests simply were not a great problem.

3

So in the past few decades, as insect and disease depredations became more serious, resulting in a high proportion of infested fruit, interest in home orcharding, even on the farm, began to wane. Of course there were those who tried to control the pests and to grow fruit. But large trees required more spraying or

Young semi-dwarf apple tree in bloom.

dusting equipment than the small farmer or "backyard gardener" had or could afford to own. Many trees were neglected; others were cut down.

The standard American fruit tree was the large type. For many home gardeners, and even on the smaller farms, these trees required too much room. Often they were overcrowded—and that resulted in fine shade, but little fruit. Obviously the large size of the standard tree has been a hindrance to enthusiasm for fruit trees on homesteads.

The Modern Dwarf

Now comes the modern dwarf to answer many of the problems that have plagued the small-scale fruit grower for many years. It has taken a long time to achieve this end, particularly with apple trees, and a good deal of hard trial-and-error work by the dwarf enthusiasts.

The character of the *roots* of a tree, called the rootstock, determines whether the tree is standard or dwarf. Until recently, dwarfing rootstocks for apples were badly mixed in this country, and some used were not suitable. Today nurserymen can use pure, *proven* rootstock varieties (also called clones) for propagating dwarf apple and pear trees. Also there is now a series of good dwarfing apple stocks so that different degrees of dwarfness are attainable. The requirements for the successful culture of dwarf trees are better understood now than formerly. For instance, it is now possible to grow small apple trees without the intricate cultural details that have always characterized European methods. Also, training fruit trees to desired forms is made more feasible as the result of utilizing the right rootstock.

Dwarf trees have many advantages, and some disadvantages, when compared with standard trees for home owner or amateur grower. First let us look at the advantages:

Dwarf trees take less space. In the space required by four standard apple trees (80 × 80 feet) you can plant as many as forty dwarf apple trees! Even the ordinary suburban "house and lot" has space for a few dwarfs.

Dwarf trees are easier to spray or dust. All fruit trees should be sprayed or dusted. Dwarf trees, particularly the little dwarfs, can be sprayed with an efficient hand sprayer or duster; the expensive, bulky equipment for standard trees is not needed. Spraying or dusting dwarfs is much easier, and consequently it gets done.

Dwarf trees bear fruit sooner. A standard apple tree usu-

Courtesy Michigan State University
Three year old Golden Delicious on dwarfing rootstock EM 26.

ally does not produce fruit for five to ten years after you set it out in your orchard. A dwarf tree will often bear fruit in two years; occasionally, *the same year!* However, for best results a good branch framework must be developed before heavy fruiting can be expected. Ample bearing surface should be assured by fostering vegetative growth during the first two or three years after planting.

Dwarf trees are easier to prune. Obviously a tree 5 to 10 feet tall is much easier to prune than a tree 25 to 30 feet tall.

Dwarf trees grow large fruit. Fruits, like turnips, need to be thinned if the biggest fruit is to be grown. Dwarf trees, where the tiny fruit can be thinned easily, often produce bigger fruit.

Dwarf trees make possible more variety. Naturally, if you can plant as many as ten dwarfs in the space required by a single standard tree, you can have up to ten various kinds or varieties of fruit, instead of one. This has another advantage—you can have early, mid-season and late fruit by selecting varieties that ripen at different times.

Dwarf trees are easier to harvest. Fruit from the smaller dwarfs may be picked from the ground without the bother and danger of using a ladder.

Dwarf trees mean less damaged fruit. Fruit dropping from the small dwarfs, particularly when the ground under the trees is mulched with straw, hay or sawdust, is often undamaged.

Dwarf trees produce top-quality fruit. Fruit produced on a dwarf tree not only tastes as good as fruit from a standard tree, but, because it is easier to give dwarfs better care, the fruit often surpasses that from large, and particularly from old, commercial trees. Fruits on dwarfs often mature earlier and color better than those on the standard large tree.

As for the disadvantages, here are several which you should know about in order to make a fair comparison:

Dwarf trees need intensive culture. They will not stand neglect. Suitable soil and good care are very important.

7

Four year old Red Delicious on EM 26.

8

Exposure to direct sunshine is essential—never plant dwarfs in the shade.

Dwarf trees may be shorter-lived. They seem to mature faster and grow old sooner. Yet with proper management, dwarf trees will live many years.

Dwarf trees may need artificial support. This is certainly true with apples on Malling IX, dwarf pears grown as bushes or little trees, and of course with most rigidly trained trees.

Some fruits are usually not dwarfed so successfully or so markedly as the apple and pear. This aspect will be considered further in the next chapter.

2

What Dwarf Trees Are

In the first chapter we brought out the fact that it is the root-stock which determines whether a tree will be a dwarf, standard size, or something between the two. When we take a look back at that statement, we learn of the wonderful success of men who have been able to develop trees which are in many ways *almost exactly what they wanted them to be.*

Unless you have had experience in growing fruit trees, you may not know that they are not grown from seeds as are common garden vegetables and flowers. For instance, if you are eating a delicious McIntosh apple and you get the idea of saving the seeds and planting them so that you will be able to have trees of that *same* delicious variety on your place, you had better reconsider. The trees you would get haven't a chance in many thousand of even closely resembling McIntosh. More than likely they would turn out to be much less desirable varieties and some might actually fail to bear any apples at all.

Trees grown from seed are called seedlings, and in the case of fruit trees, seedlings do not "come true." Just why this is so is rather difficult to explain in a few words. Briefly, it is due to a complex chromosomal or genetic makeup. There are practically innumerable possible combinations of the genes—the inheritance factors—hence almost unlimited chances for variability in seedling characteristics.

Our forefathers used seedling trees very widely to supply their families with home-grown fruit. Some of the seedlings bore good fruit; many more produced very inferior fruit which could be used only for cider, perhaps. Oftentimes, when an early American farmer or amateur horticulturist did find a seedling tree that produced good fruit, he would let his friends take twigs or shoots to graft onto their own inferior trees. This is called

A section of Malling IX rootstock taken from a propagating stool bed. The shoots are separated from the parent and planted in rows for later budding to varieties.

top-grafting, a kind of vegetative or clonal propagation. The result is a tree with roots from one source and a top—the whole of the tree above the ground or at least a limb—from another source.

Vegetative or clonal propagation simply means propagation without seeds. Top-grafting is one kind; let us consider another kind which consists of taking a piece of a root or a rooted shoot (a "sucker") originating from the root system and transplanting it to another location. If it grows, the tree that develops will be a duplicate of the "mother" plant. This is very similar to the transplanting of raspberry suckers. *Clonal* rootstocks for fruit trees are vegetatively propagated rootstocks. In contrast to apple

This illustrates the difference in characteristics between the rootstock and top or scion of a dwarf apple. *Left:* A shoot has developed directly from the rootstock; *right* is the scion which has been budded onto the rootstock. Note the contrast in leaves; if the shoot from the rootstock were allowed to grow, the apples, if any were borne, would not be edible.

seedling rootstocks which, as we have seen, vary so widely in vigor, *all clonal rootstocks from one plant are essentially alike.*

Just as a variety like McIntosh is propagated vegetatively aboveground in order to preserve its tree and fruit characteristics for future generations of trees, so a clonal rootstock like the dwarf Malling IX is propagated to provide more rootstocks with the same good dwarfing characteristics. Since it is possible to unite by budding—a type of grafting—a true McIntosh top (or "scion") with a true dwarfing root, a tree with the desirable characteristics of both is the result.

Although the actual antiquity of dwarf apple tree culture is not exactly known, it is conjectured that at some time someone

Apple tree on Malling 9 dwarfing rootstock which grew large instead of remaining dwarfed. The reason, as seen here, is that the tree was planted too deeply, which caused a large root (the man's hand is on it) to grow *above* the dwarf rootstock.

must have taken notice of certain dwarf apple seedlings. Perhaps these trees remained small even as they matured. Probably it was also found that these particular trees suckered and the suckers could be rooted. Here was a source of needed rootstocks. When buds or twigs were grafted onto these rootstocks they developed and produced fruit earlier than normally. *Furthermore, the trees remained small.* Such trees must have attracted considerable attention. As a matter of fact, dwarf fruit trees have been popular in Europe for many years.

Today to get dwarf fruit trees of your own, you do not have to propagate them yourself unless you prefer to. Ordinarily, you buy dwarfs two to three years old—after they have been successfully budded and grown into small nursery trees. But it is important that you understand what you are buying. The lower part or *rootstock* of a dwarf fruit tree is usually, as we have seen, a special dwarf variety. Its top part or scion, the part that produces the fruit, can be one of several well-known varieties of good fruit—whichever you choose. Different varieties of dwarf rootstock produce trees of different heights, ranging from about 5 feet to 20 feet. At present the smallest available dwarf apple tree (5 to 10 feet at maturity) is produced by the *Malling IX* rootstock. This variety of rootstock is said to be *very dwarfing* or *extremely dwarfing* another such rootstock is MM 26.

There are many other dwarf rootstocks which produce trees of different sizes. You may hear them called *medium dwarfs* or *semi-dwarfs* (approximately 10 to 15 feet), or *semi-standards* (approximately 15 to 20 feet). Note comparative size of mature McIntosh apple trees grown on several rootstocks in the chart on page 17.

3

What Is a Good Dwarf?

Not all dwarf fruit trees are alike. There is quite a difference in the various types you may be offered at different nurseries. Some should never be called dwarfs for they grow almost as large as standard trees. Others—true dwarfs—are from 5 to 12 feet tall at maturity. If you buy from a nursery that specializes in dwarfs and keeps informed of the latest developments, you can be pretty sure of getting true dwarfs and good ones. You should always find out what the rootstock is. Also see to it that no roots are growing from above the bud union—recognizable as a small bulge or crook in the trunk just above ground. (See Figure 4 on page 40.)

With apples, as we have seen, it is important that the rootstock should be a clonal stock rather than a seedling, because in clonal propagation, every individual rootstock of a particular selection has exactly the same inherent makeup. Hence all McIntosh buds worked on Malling IX rootstocks, for example, will develop into dwarf apple trees very closely similar in small size and early bearing. When propagated on clonal rootstocks, we can rather accurately prophesy just what trees will do.

SOME GOOD ROOTSTOCKS FOR APPLES

We formerly knew of two dwarfing apple rootstocks in this country—the Paradise and the Doucin. Under these two names several different rootstock varieties were distributed and used as

15

stocks for dwarf trees. Often two or more different types were mixed. In recent years these mixtures have been straightened out, and nurserymen can now use pure rootstock varieties for growing dwarf trees. Since many of the dwarf apple rootstock investigations were carried out by Dr. R. G. Hatton at the East Malling Research Station, East Malling, Kent, England, the clonal rootstocks now largely used for dwarfing apple varieties are known as Malling stocks. Today the best known rootstock for growing very dwarf apple trees is Malling IX. Malling Merton 26 has more recently shown promise. Malling IX is also known as Jaune de Metz. Malling VIII, which is the old Paradise, has similar dwarfing capabilities, but is not considered to be as acceptable a stock as Malling IX or MM 26.

Another dwarf stock is under study in Iowa and appears highly promising. Sometimes called the Clark dwarf (in deference to its discoverer), it may be used as an intermediate stem piece between the root and the top variety. It then effectively dwarfs the top. Several varieties are reported to make productive dwarf trees when worked in this fashion. An added feature is the winter-hardiness of this stock.

Malling I, II, III, IV, V, VI, and VII are all dwarfing stocks, but not to the degree of Malling VIII and IX. Trees propagated on any of these seven stocks will be dwarfed to a certain extent. The ultimate size of trees may vary from less than one half to about three quarters that of standard seedling-rooted trees. Malling I is a promising rootstock for commercial plantings. Malling III suckers badly, and as a result is not too highly regarded. Malling IV is one of the better, semi-dwarfing stocks, but has a serious weakness—it makes a poor union with some varieties, and the trees often suffer badly from breakage at or near the union. Malling V is used to some extent while experience with Malling VI is very meager. Arranged in order of vigor with the most vigorous varieties first, the most promising of these seven rootstocks are probably Malling I, V, II, and VII. Much investiga-

SIZE-CONTROLLING APPLE TREE ROOTSTOCKS

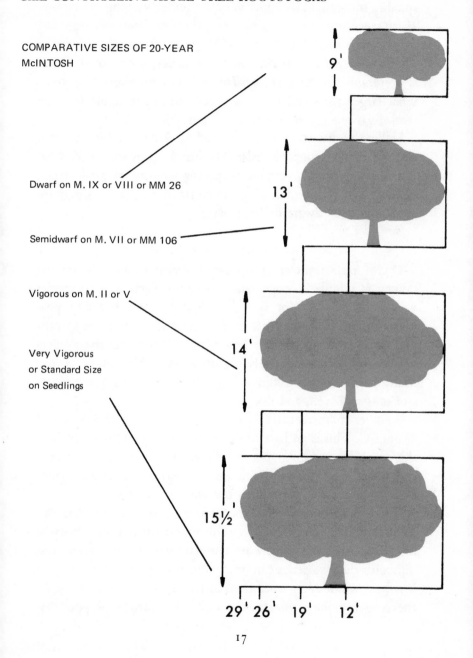

COMPARATIVE SIZES OF 20-YEAR
McINTOSH

9'

Dwarf on M. IX or VIII or MM 26

13'

Semidwarf on M. VII or MM 106

Vigorous on M. II or V

14'

Very Vigorous
or Standard Size
on Seedlings

15½'

29' 26' 19' 12'

tional work is needed to establish which rootstocks are the more suitable for individual apple varieties under varying conditions. *With weak-growing apple varieties, some of these semi-dwarfing stocks, such as Malling VII, perhaps, may be more suitable than the extremely dwarfing Malling IX. Usually, however, the latter is preferable for the small garden tree.* For those desiring somewhat larger trees and for commercial orchards, apple trees on semi-dwarfing rootstocks may be desirable.

Malling 26 has recently performed as well as Malling IX as a very dwarfing rootstock. Also Malling Merton stocks MM106 and MM111 are proving excellent for semi-dwarf apple trees. Malling XII, XIII and XVI produce standard size trees and are not suitable for dwarf orchard plantings.

A GOOD ROOTSTOCK FOR PEARS

Dwarf pear trees are propagated almost exclusively on the quince (Cydonia oblonga mill.), which dwarfs many varieties very successfully. Not only is the degree of dwarfing pronounced, but the trees grow much less upright and more spreading in form. Probably the best type of quince is the Angers variety, which is moderately vigorous, and which roots readily. Many pear varieties make good unions with Angers quince rootstocks—grow well, and live long.

Another more recently introduced quince rootstock is called Quince C. This is an East Malling designation and differentiates this clone from the Angers or Quince A. Trials have indicated that varieties on this rootstock are less vigorous, produce smaller trees, and are well adapted to training on trellises.

Unfortunately, some common varieties, such as Bartlett and Winter Nelis, do not make a good union with Angers because of a lack of compatibility or congeniality. To overcome this difficulty these varieties can be *double-worked*. Double-working involves two budding operations instead of a single one. First, on the Angers quince rootstock is budded a variety of pear that

Dwarf pear tree.

will make a good union, such as Hardy. Then, on Hardy—after it grows into a shoot—is budded the desired variety of pear, such as Bartlett. Although Bartlett might not have formed a good union with the quince rootstock it will do perfectly well on Hardy in this manner. Angers quince rootstock provides the roots, Hardy forms the intermediate stem piece, and Bartlett produces the pears.

In general, dwarf pears have not been so widely grown in this country as in Europe. However, since a standard pear tree often grows 20 to 25 feet tall, the need for a dwarf pear is pretty well justified. In the next few years you may find still more nurseries developing these dwarf pears and making them available to home growers.

SOME ROOTSTOCKS FOR OTHER FRUITS

Although it is perfectly possible to grow many fruits besides apples and pears as dwarf trees, there has not been nearly so much interest in doing so. One reason for this is that most other fruit trees, with the exception of sweet cherries, are already fairly small. The peach, apricot, nectarine, plum, sour cherry, and quince are usually little more than half the size of a standard McIntosh apple tree. Also, it is comparatively easy to prune down the stone fruit trees, keeping them low and small—much more so than is usually possible with apples and pears. Another reason is that the standard stone fruit trees will often bear fruit two or three years after planting, whereas the standard apple trees usually take much longer. However, there are certain rootstocks which may be used to dwarf these stone fruits somewhat, and some nurserymen have them available. *It should be noted that, when allowed to grow more or less naturally, differences in vigor and fruiting are usually not nearly so great between dwarf and standard stone fruit trees as between dwarf and standard apple and pear trees.*

The peach, as a rule, is not well grown as a dwarf tree unless trained to a special form. On certain rootstocks reasonably satisfactory results have sometimes been obtained. The apricot (Prunus Armeniaca L.), Myrobalan plum (Prunus cerasifera Ehrh.), Marianna (Prunus cerasifera X P. Munsoniana), Saint Julien plum (Prunus domestica, var. insititia B.) and western sand cherry (Prunus Besseyi B.) have all been used to some

Courtesy N. Y. State Agri. Exp. Station

The sweet cherry variety Giant after five seasons of growth in the orchard row, bench-grafted at 26 inches above the root. A. On Mahaleb. B. On Mazzard.

extent as dwarfing rootstocks for peaches. Standard peaches are grown on peach seedling roots and are often perfectly satisfactory for the home garden. With proper pruning technique, small size can be maintained fairly satisfactorily.

The nectarine is sometimes propagated for dwarfing purposes on Prunus Besseyi B. and sometimes on almond (Prunus communis Fritsch). Usual commercial propagation is on peach seedling roots.

Dwarf apricot is grown largely on Prunus Besseyi B. or Saint Julien while the standard rootstocks are peach, apricot and myrobalan plum.

Sweet cherry varieties may be dwarfed in some cases by propagating on the common Mahaleb (Prunus Mahaleb L.). Also the use of sour cherry (Prunus Cerasus L.) rootstocks has been reported to dwarf the sweet cherry and to induce early

Courtesy Michigan State University

Row of Golden Delicious on EM VII, a semi-dwarfing rootstock, in the fifth year.

bearing. The Mazzard or wild sweet cherry rootstock produces large long-lived trees. There is a difference of opinion as to the probable success that may be expected in attempting to dwarf sweet cherries. A recent report indicates that the best way to obtain dwarf sweet cherry trees is to graft the desired variety onto Mahaleb seedlings which have been allowed to attain a height of 26 inches before grafting. The long Mahaleb stem appears to exert a dwarfing effect on the top-worked variety so that the dwarfness is comparable to dwarf apple trees.

For sour cherries, the following dwarfing rootstocks have been used: the sand cherry (Prunus pumila L.), the western sand cherry (Prunus Besseyi B.) and the Stockton Morello. Mahaleb is usually considered to dwarf sour cherries, but often trees on this stock grow quite vigorously. A long Mahaleb stem (as described under sweet cherry) should probably be used.

Plums usually do not require dwarfing rootstocks and are grown mostly on Myrobalan plum (Prunus cerasifera Ehrh.) or peach (Prunus Persica S. & B.). The sand cherries (Prunus pumila L. and P. Besseyi B.) and St. Julien plum have occasionally been used for dwarfing purposes. St. Julien C is a good clonal strain.

Quince trees are grown as small trees or bushes and are propagated on Angers Quince or other quince rootstocks.

There is considerable investigational work directed toward improving dwarfing stocks for the various fruits, and further developments are to be expected.

4

Planning a Dwarf Orchard

On the next few pages you will find five simple tables which should give you much of the information you need to plan your own fruit orchard. The temptation is to start buying trees and setting them out before you have a good plan in mind and a good layout. Once the trees are planted it is not always easy to move them and you may spend years trying to correct your early mistakes. This will not happen, however, if you give careful consideration to your problem beforehand, keeping in mind the five basic considerations covered in the tables. These five considerations are:

(1) Space requirements
(2) Probable yield
(3) Ripening timetable
(4) Suggested uses for different varieties
(5) Cross pollination needs

Take a look first at the table showing the usual space requirements for the various types of trees. As you can see, space is not much of a problem. Almost every home has room for at least a half-dozen dwarf trees. There is room for six or eight dwarf apple trees in the spread of a single well-grown standard apple or sweet cherry. Even if you don't have this much space you may be able to grow some espaliers, or cordons (see chapter 13), along a building or wall, or possibly as a decorative fence. Simple upright cordons are sometimes set as close as one foot apart, but such trees require very specialized attention and will be considered later on. The table below gives the approximate space requirements for the different trees in reasonably good soil. This information should serve as a rough guide in planning your orchard. The space figures are given in round numbers and deviations will often have to be made. In some cases wider spacing may be required in all categories.

FRUIT TREE SPACE REQUIREMENTS

Apple (dwarfed on Malling IX rootstock)	12' × 12'
Apple (semi-dwarf)	20' × 20'
Apple (standard)	40' × 40'
Pear (dwarf)	12' × 12'
Pear (standard)	20' × 20'
Quince	12' × 12'
Other fruit trees (dwarf)	12' × 12'
Other fruit trees (standard)	20' × 20'

In considering a possible location or space for your dwarf fruit trees, keep these two ideas in mind:

(1) Direct sunshine is vital to satisfactory tree growth and fruiting. Fruit trees in even partial shade are likely to fruit sparingly.

(2) Low areas, particularly where there is no opportunity for air drainage to lower levels, may be entirely unsuited as dwarf orchard sites because of the probability of damage to blossoms and young fruits by spring frosts. Air temperatures 3 or 4 degrees below freezing can be disastrous at the critical blooming and fruit-setting period.

After you have figured out how many trees you can plant in the space you have available, you should consider the probable yield of fruit. Remember that it is almost as much trouble to care for half a dozen trees as it is to look after several times that number. On the other hand, you will not want to be burdened with more fruit than you can normally use. Estimate just how much of each fruit you can use including canning and whatever amount you would like to give to friends, or sell. Then study the next table and determine how many trees of each variety to plant to get the desired amount of fruit. You will probably figure on the basis of satisfactory growth and production. Con-

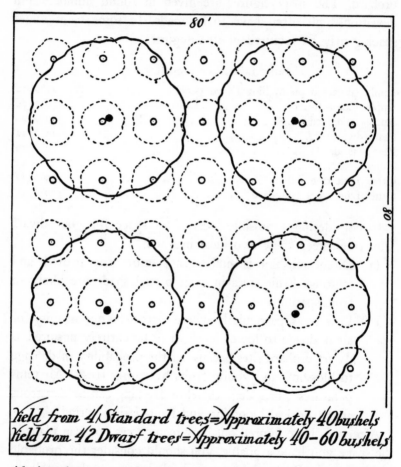

Yield from 4 Standard trees = Approximately 40 bushels
Yield from 42 Dwarf trees = Approximately 40-60 bushels

sidering the many uncertainties involved in growing tree fruits, it may be wise to overestimate your needs to some extent.

The figures given in this table are conservative, and should be considered approximate only. Soil conditions, the care and attention given to the trees and other factors are subject to wide variation from place to place. Also, different varieties vary tremendously, both in earliness of bearing and in production.

ESTIMATED PROBABLE YIELD OF DWARF FRUIT TREES

Kind of fruit tree	Years after orchard planting to first fruiting *	Bushel yield of mature trees *
Apple (on Malling IX)	2 or 3	1
Apple (on semi-dwarf stock)	4 or 5	5
Pear	3	1
Peach	3	2
Plum (Japanese)	3	1
Plum (European)	4	1
Cherry (sour)	3	1
Cherry (sweet)	5	1
Quince	4	1
Nectarine	3	1
Apricot	3	1

* Approximate.

The next thing to consider is the ripening timetable. Usually you do not want too much fruit ripening at one time. This can be avoided by planting the right varieties, and with apples by planting summer, fall and winter sorts which will give a harvest over the maximum possible period. We would like to give you a table showing the approximate dates of ripening but of course this is not practicable because seasons vary so much in different parts of the country. Therefore, we have simply listed some of the better varieties in the *order of ripening*. Those in italics are especially suitable for home planting. It is admitted that other horticulturists probably would differ somewhat in choice of varieties.

From this table you can easily draw up a specific ripening timetable for your locality by finding out approximate ripening dates of varieties best grown in your section from your nursery or your state agricultural college.

DWARF FRUIT RIPENING TIMETABLE

(Fruits ripen approximately in the order listed)

Apple — *Lodi, Duchess, Melba, Quinto, Beacon, Early McIntosh,* Gravenstein, *Paulared, Wealthy, McIntosh, Cortland, Macoun, Spartan, Cox Orange, Jonathan,* Wagener, *Red Delicious,* Stayman, *Golden Delicious, Red Rome, Northern or Red Spy,* Golden Russet.

Pear — Tyson, *Clapp Favorite, Bartlett,* Flemish Beauty, *Seckel, Worden Seckel,* Howell, Duchess, Conference, *Sheldon, Dana Hovey, Anjou, Bosc,* Easter, Kieffer (for storage), *Winter Nelis.*

Peach — *Marigold, Garnet Beauty, Rich-haven, Glohaven, Redhaven, Golden Jubilee, Triogem,* Golden East, Vedette, *Halehaven,* Valiant, Elberta.

Plum — *Shiro* (Japanese), Bradshaw, *Formosa* (Japanese), Santa Rosa (Japanese), Burbank (Japanese), *Washington, Pearl, Imperial Epineuse, Imperial Gage, German Prune,* Italian Prune, *Stanley,* Hall, *Bavay or Reine Claude,* Shropshire (Damson), *Albion,* President.

Sweet Cherry — Seneca, Early Rivers, *Black Tartarian,* Yellow Spanish, *Napoleon* (sometimes called *Royal Anne*), *Schmidt,* Bing, *Windsor,* Gold, *Lambert.*

Sour Cherry — Early Richmond, *Montmorency, English Morello.*

Duke Cherry — Olivet, *Reine Hortense, Royal Duke.*

Nectarine — Goldmine, *Rivers Orange,* Garden State, Hunter, *Sure Crop.* (Nectarine trees are very similar to peach trees. The fruits are smaller; the flavor is different, and the skin is smooth, like a plum.)

Apricot — Montgamet, Early Golden, Moorpark, Geneva. (Apricots are very successfully grown in the West and in favorable situations may be quite satisfactory in other sections. It is important to remember that apricots bloom early when weather conditions may be unfavorable for pollination and fruit-setting. Blossoms are often destroyed by spring frosts and hence protected locations are essential for success, particularly in the northeast and middle-western areas.)

Quince — *Orange, Champion.* (Quinces are used principally for preserves, jams and jellies. However, the trees are considered as ornaments on many lawns.)

Of course, different varieties do not behave alike in different parts of the country. Those that do well in New England are often not successfully grown in the fruit sections of Virginia or Missouri, for example. In general, the varieties listed here can be grown in the northeast, from the Middle Atlantic area north through New England and west to the Mississippi River, as well as in the Pacific northwest. Remember that the peach is limited to sections where the winter temperature does not normally fall much below minus 15 degrees F. The nectarine is similarly limited and the apricot is very sensitive to spring frosts.

After you have considered which varieties to plant from a time-of-ripening standpoint, it is important to remember that different varieties of fruits have different best uses. Thus, some apples are best for eating out of hand, some for baking, some for salads, some for sauce, etc. Many varieties are excellent all-purpose sorts. Some plum or prune varieties make a better canned product than others. The same is true for pears and peaches. To get the most from your dwarf fruit planting you should become well acquainted with the uses to which the different varieties of tree fruits grown in your locality are best suited.

SUGGESTED VARIETIES FOR DIFFERENT USES

(This is a personal selection and is not intended to be complete or "authoritative.")

Apple —Cooking: Crimson Beauty, Duchess, Wealthy, McIntosh, Cortland, Rhode Island Greening, Baldwin, Gallia, Gravenstein.
Salad; eat out of hand: Cortland, Golden Delicious, Northern Spy, Melba, Early McIntosh, Gravenstein, McIntosh, Macoun, Fameuse, Cox Orange, Delicious, Jonathan, Stayman.

Plums —Canned: German Prune, Italian Prune, Stanley, Hall, Shropshire Damson.
Eat out of hand: Formosa, Pearl, Imperial Epineuse, Albion, Bavay.

Pears —Canned: Bartlett, Gorham, Seckel.
Eat out of hand: Bartlett, Gorham, Seckel, Conference, Sheldon, Dana Hovey, Bosc, Winter Nelis.

Peaches—All except possibly the early varieties are luscious for eating out of hand and for canning.

Ten-year-old dwarf Wealthy trees in full bloom.

One more factor needs consideration—the pollination problem. Some varieties are *self-fruitful*. This means that the blossoms of such a variety can be fertilized by the pollen of the same variety. On the other hand, many varieties are *self-unfruitful*. This means that they will not bear fruit unless fertilized by the pollen of a *different* variety. So to be sure of getting fruit you must have another variety near them. Bees, particularly honey bees, are the main pollen distributors. A hive of bees, in fact, may increase your orchard yield considerably. For this reason it is important to be careful in using insecticides that kill bees. Hand pollination of blossoms can be done successfully and holds some promise for growers of dwarf fruits, but it involves certain technical details. The best way to learn more about this is from your state college or experiment station. Hand pollination of hundreds of acres of commercial apple orchards in the northwest has been remarkably successful. Usually you will not need to worry about pollination so long as you plant two or more varieties of each fruit. The table below will give you some helpful information.

POLLINATION REQUIREMENTS OF THE DIFFERENT FRUITS

Apples —Mostly self-unfruitful. (A red bud sport of any variety will not pollinize that variety. Baldwin, Gravenstein, Rhode Island Greening and Stayman produce poor pollen, and hence should not be planted for cross-pollination purposes.)

Pears —Mostly self-unfruitful. (Seckel and Bartlett will not pollinate each other.)

Peaches —Mostly self-fruitful. (This means that a single Elberta peach tree, for example, will set fruit. J. H. Hale is not self-fruitful.)

Plums —Many varieties self-unfruitful.

Sweet Cherries—Self-unfruitful. (Furthermore, Bing, Napoleon and Lambert will not pollinate each other.)

Sour Cherries —Self-fruitful.

Duke Cherries—Self-unfruitful.

Quinces —Self-fruitful.

31

Now that you have considered everything in the five tables above, you are ready to make a layout for your own dwarf orchard. Perhaps it seems unnecessary to you to do this just for a small dwarf orchard. However, we think you will save a lot of time and get better results if you do. Remember, it is much easier to erase pencil marks from a piece of paper than to rearrange planted trees. Simply take a sheet of ordinary paper and draw a rough plan view of your house and the land around it, showing the approximate dimensions. Then with a different colored pencil mark the spots where you want to grow dwarf trees. Use the space requirement table for proper distances. If you live in a cold climate peach trees should be in the most sheltered areas near the house. Remember that spraying and pruning will be a little easier if your trees are more or less near each other. And be sure you do not put your trees where they are likely to be damaged by cars, livestock or children. Plan your dwarf orchard to suit the appearance of your homestead as well as the fruit needs of your family. *Do not plant fruit trees in the shade or too close to shade trees. They need sunlight.*

Here is a suggested dwarf orchard for a productive country home. This orchard of twenty-six trees requires an area of approximately 50 × 100 feet or slightly larger and may yield up to 25 bushels of fruit per year:

8 Apple
5 Pear
4 Peach
3 Plum
2 Sweet Cherry
1 Sour Cherry
1 Quince
1 Nectarine
1 Apricot

5

How to Buy or Propagate Your Own Dwarf Trees

You have a choice between buying young dwarf trees from a nursery or propagating them yourself at home. Here are some facts to help you decide which to do. If you buy the trees from a nursery, you spend money for trees ready to set out. If you grow them yourself it will cost less but it will also take several years longer to get fruit. Starting from rootstocks ready for budding, it takes two to four years to grow high grade dwarf trees. Espaliers and rigidly trained dwarfs often take six or more years of exacting work. So by buying them ready to plant you get a head start of several years.

NURSERY-GROWN TREES

Be sure to buy from a reliable nursery and one that specializes in dwarf trees. A place that has not specialized may not be up-to-date on the best rootstocks and the newest developments in the field. With dwarf fruit trees, these new developments in the past few years have been very important. You may be able to get some good advice on finding a reliable nursery from your state college of agriculture or experiment station. Also be sure to visit the various nurseries and see what kind of work they do. You can learn a lot this way. Incidentally, it is a good idea to place a spring planting order some time in January or February, well in advance of the planting season.

There is a wonderful satisfaction in growing your own dwarf trees, provided you have the knowledge of what to do, the perseverance to do it, and the patience to await results. It is certainly true that many folks just like to grow trees from scratch, so to speak. Furthermore, certain desirable home varieties can be obtained in no other way. Here are the necessary directions:

(1) *Importance of rootstock.* The importance of the rootstock cannot be overstressed, particularly with dwarf apples and pears. Much unhappy experience has proved that this portion of a dwarf tree must receive most careful consideration. Past failures have been due in no small measure to inadequate appreciation of rootstock. It is the rootstock that determines whether a tree will be naturally dwarfed, and also whether a tree can be successfully trellis-trained. Dwarf apple rootstocks need particular emphasis. *The home gardener should have clearly in mind that MIX, 26 or possibly VII are the best very-dwarfing rootstocks for most apple varieties.* In purchasing garden trees from a nursery be sure that the rootstock, as well as the top variety, is true-to-name. Many so-called "dwarf" apple trees sold recently are apparently growing to full size. This probably means one of two things. Either the top variety has been allowed to form its own roots, or else the rootstock was not Malling IX or any other very-dwarfing rootstock.

First, if you are producing your own dwarfs, the proper dwarfing rootstocks must be obtained. These rootstocks are listed in chapter 3. To obtain the few rootstocks that are needed by the average home-gardener is often not too easy. Probably your state college department of horticulture or your local nurseryman can best advise you of sources of stock. If the desired rootstocks are obtained, they can be "lined out" in almost any location that will grow a good general garden. By "lining out" is meant setting about 8 inches apart in rows 3½ to 4 feet apart. This is done usually early in the spring, and preferably as soon as the soil can be worked satisfactorily. With the advent of favorable growing weather, these rootstocks will leaf out and begin to grow. If growth is sufficient, budding can be done in late July or in August of the same year. However, it may be necessary to delay budding until the next summer, because of the small size of the stocks (they should be at least ¼ inch in diameter at the point of budding), or because of poor vigor, which may result in failure of the bark to "slip" properly—separate from the wood as part of the normal growth process.

(2) *Budding*. There are several different ways of budding. The way we suggest is accomplished late in July or August and is called *shield budding*. Here is how it is done: With a sharp knife, make a T-shaped cut in the bark of the stock, about 4 to 6 inches above the ground. Then open up the flaps of bark slightly. Into this T, slip a *shield bud* which has been cut from a new shoot of the desired variety. Then tie the bud with special rubber bands, raffia or string, to hold the living tissues of the bud in close contact with those of the rootstock, and to prevent desiccation or serious drying out. The tying material encircles the stock just above and just below the inserted bud. After ten days to two weeks, the ties can be cut away, as the union of stock and bud is then completed. The technique in budding is very important but not at all difficult to master.

Now here is how to obtain the shield bud just mentioned. Most growing shoots have rather evenly spaced leaves, and in the angle of each leaf stem is a bud or growing point, which is potentially a new plant of the same variety. With a sharp knife, the leaf is cut off, leaving about ½ inch of leaf stem (petiole). Then the bud shield is obtained by making a shallow slicing cut from a little below to a little above the actual bud. The shield then is simply a shield-shaped (roughly speaking) piece of bark, with the bud and leaf stem in approximately the center. Often a little actual wood is taken, depending on the depth of the cut.

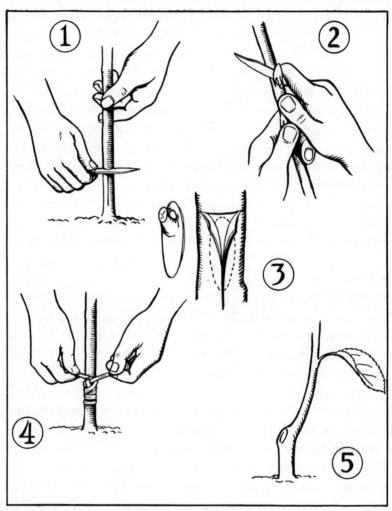

1. A "T-cut" is made in the stem of the dwarf stock. 2. A shield bud is cut from a budding stick, a branch of a popular variety of fruit. 3. The shield is ready to be inserted in the T-cut. 4. The bud is tied with raffia or a rubber band which should be removed after two weeks. 5. Early next spring the dwarf stock stem is cut off just above the inserted bud and this bud then will grow into an upright "whip" or single shoot to form the basis of the new dwarf tree. Note photo of actual budding operation on next page.

It is very important in budding to keep cut tissues from drying out, and to complete each budding operation without undue delay. In fact, *preventing moisture loss is one of the most important things to remember.*

(3) *Growing the young tree.* The bud, now nicely united with the rootstock, remains dormant until the following spring.

The author buds Malling rootstocks. In his left hand is the budstick from which buds are cut. With his right hand, he inserts a bud into the T-cut with the back of the knife blade. On the left are two rootstocks with inserted buds tied in place. The following spring, the top of the rootstock will be cut off just above the inserted bud which will grow to form the new top.

Occasionally it will grow somewhat during the fall, but this is not usual nor desirable. Just before resumption of growth in the spring, you must cut off the rootstock just above the inserted bud. This gives the bud the top or uppermost position on the stock, and if it has wintered successfully, it should grow vigorously. From time to time all other growths from the stock are rubbed or pruned off, so that the entire vigor of the tree is shunted into the one shoot (which has developed from the bud inserted the previous summer). Fruit trees will often grow enough in one year so that you can transplant them in the fall or the following spring, but sometimes three or more years may be required to develop proper framework and sufficient size.

Early the next spring, before growth starts, you should prune your trees. It is important to head dwarf trees low (cut back vertical growth to keep the tree short) and in some cases to grow them as bushes rather than as conventional modified leader type trees. All you have to do is *keep* them headed low and then prune them just as you would other fruit trees. (Full instructions on pruning are given in chapter 7.) *Remember to keep the bud union at least 1 to 2 inches above ground.* Otherwise, roots may develop from the top variety as explained in the next chapter.

Newly planted apple tree on dwarfing rootstock in a backyard. Note the graft union is above the ground to prevent scion rooting and subsequent loss of the dwarfing character of the tree. The depression around the trunk facilitates watering during the first year.

6

Special Directions for Planting Dwarfs

Unfortunately trees are frequently harmed or even ruined by improper care or lack of care after they are received from the nurseryman. This is easily avoided. First of all, you should dig holes for planting and have them ready to receive the young trees before they arrive. As soon as received, trees should be unwrapped and unpacked. If the roots seem to be dry, they should be moistened thoroughly with a sprinkling can or a hose. High pressures from nozzles should be avoided because of danger of injury to the roots. It may be of considerable benefit to wet down the entire tree roots, stem and branches.

Under no circumstances should nursery tree roots be unduly exposed to the air, and especially to freezing temperature, drying winds or direct sunlight. Exposure for a short period may result in irreparable damage to the roots, with consequent poor tree performance or total failure. In case there should be some delay in planting, there are several good ways to keep the trees in good condition until they can be planted or set out in permanent locations. Of course the quicker the planting can be done the better.

(1) The tree may be placed in a cool, moist cellar or protected shed, and the roots thoroughly soaked with water, and kept covered with moist dirt or wet straw, burlap or other blanketing. The coverings must be kept moist.

(2) They can be partially buried in cool, moist sawdust in an icehouse.

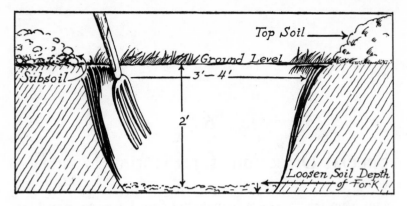

1. A hole is dug considerably wider and deeper than the tree roots.

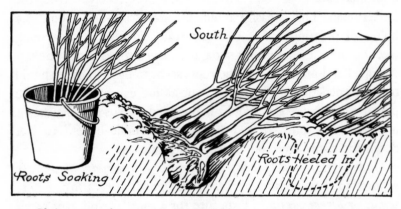

2. If the roots of trees as they arrive from the nursery seem at all dry they should be soaked. If not planted immediately, trees should be "heeled in."

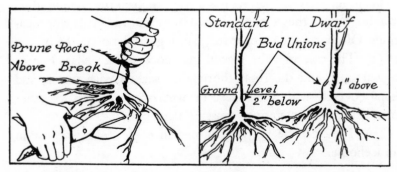

3. Any damaged roots should be pruned with a clean cut. 4. For standard trees bud unions are below ground; for dwarfs, above.

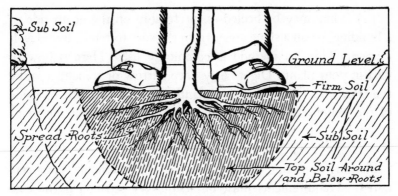

5. Shovel the best soil immediately below and around the roots and tramp firmly to avoid air pockets.

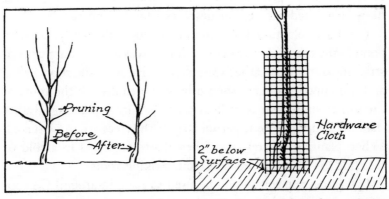

6. Prune (see directions in Chapter 7).

7. Circle tree with hardware cloth against rodents.

8. Place a hay or straw mulch around the tree.

9. Stake apple trees, which are weak at the bud union.

(3) They may be heeled-in, preferably on the north side of a building, or on a slope away from the sun, to retard bud development. This last method is commonly used. Here is how to heel-in your plants. Dig a fairly deep furrow or trench; separate the trees and place them in a slanting position against one side of the trench. Then replace the soil and firm it about the roots.

PLANTING

Planting or setting dwarf fruit trees is not difficult, yet a certain few requirements must be adequately satisfied if the best results are to be obtained.

(1) *The trees and particularly the roots should not be allowed to dry out at all prior to the actual planting operation.* This has been mentioned before, but deserves added emphasis.

(2) Each planting hole should be dug sufficiently large to contain the entire root system without breaking, bending or constricting any roots. Larger trees may arrive with the roots balled and burlapped, and care should be taken to disturb the roots or the soil around them as little as possible during planting. Rather shallow planting is best, particularly if the trees are to be staked. When planting several trees, they may be carried in a fold of wet burlap—this prevents sun from striking roots.

(3) Good top soil should be used to pack in around the root system. In certain instances with heavy clay soils, the use of wet peat moss mixed with the soil has stimulated initial tree growth.

(4) The soil should be thoroughly moist—but not waterlogged. Often, watering, using about a pailful to a tree, results in better contact of roots with the soil.

(5) Pack the soil closely around the roots with your fingers —leave no air pockets. Cover roots with 3 or 4 inches of soil before treading it down with your feet. Excessive tamping of balled and burlapped trees should be avoided.

(6) *Especially with dwarf apples and pears, after leveling the soil, the union of rootstock and top variety—usually evident as a*

42

bulge—should be slightly above the surface. This is extremely important. If the union is down in the soil, the top variety will send out roots (scion rooting), the tree will gradually become "own-rooted" above the dwarf rootstock, and a large tree will result.

(7) The use of fertilizer at planting time, or during the first growing season, is not recommended. Definite *harm* will often result from this practice. It is always the best plan to have the soil in good condition—both tilth and fertility—before setting out an orchard.

(8) Newly planted one- and two-year-old trees should usually be pruned back more or less severely, depending on the particular type or shape of dwarf tree desired. To grow little trees of the apple, adequate pruning may consist simply of thinning out excessive branches, and possibly shortening of some shoots. To develop bushes, low pruning or heading-back is required—shortening of all upper growth. Peach, nectarine and sweet cherry trees are usually pruned more severely than apples and pears at planting time.

(9) Tying to supports should be done immediately after setting trained dwarf trees. At least by the second growing season, Malling IX trees, grown as little trees, should be tied to stakes. (See page 56, concerning staking.)

(10) *The menace to your dwarf fruit trees from mice and rabbits is a real one and should be kept in mind constantly.* One-fourth-inch-mesh hardware cloth may be cut and formed into suitable cylinders to protect the lower trunks. Special poison baits may be used very successfully when applied in mouse runs or tunnel paths, particularly under a hay mulch.

Fencing the entire orchard against rabbits is practical where dwarf trees are planted in a compact block. Chicken wire may be used and need be in place only during fall and winter months when rabbits are most troublesome.

Repellent paints are available, but none has proven entirely satisfactory. If rodents become a problem, detailed information on poisons and methods of application are available from the Division of Rodent Control, Fish and Wildlife Service, U. S. Department of Interior, which has conveniently located branch offices in many states, as well as trained field men. Your agricultural extension service can also be of help.

Poultry sometimes damage fruit trees by pecking at the bark. In some cases, large trees have been completely girdled and thus killed.

Little trees are fun for little boys and little girls.

7

Pruning the Dwarf Orchard

Pruning is simply cutting out parts of trees and is done to help shape or train the tree, to thin out crowding branches, to stimulate new growth, to aid fruit set and regularity in production, and to facilitate certain orchard practices such as spraying, dusting, thinning and harvesting.

Just about one hundred years ago A. J. Downing in *Fruits and Fruit Trees of America* emphasized his cardinal principle of pruning as follows: "Every fruit tree, grown in the open orchard or garden as a common standard, should be allowed to take its natural form, the whole efforts of the pruner going no further than to take out all weak and crowded branches."

From the time of Downing to the present, literally hundreds of ideas and practices concerning pruning have been fostered by well-meaning horticulturists, both professional and amateur. But the fact remains that Downing's principle is basically sound. With certain refinements, it is the basis for the pruning practices outlined here for the "little tree" type of dwarf fruit tree.

If pruning, then, has seemed a formidable project, one for the experts and the experienced, it is well to keep Downing's simple, cardinal principle in mind, together with the more important principle that good management resulting in good growth of the orchard is even more significant than pruning.

It is also well to remember that if you plant trees that have been three or more years in the nursery, the first important pruning job has usually been done for you—that which has to

A modified leader specimen of Golden Delicious apple on dwarf
stock. It has already borne considerable fruit and now requires only the
pruning of excess shoots.

do with establishing the basic branch framework of the tree.

Here are a few definitions and explanations which will help to make the remainder of this chapter easy to follow:

Shoots are any new growths; in a very young tree, even the main limbs may be referred to as "shoots."

Spurs are short—usually 1- to 3-inch—fruit-bearing shoots on pear, apple and other trees. You may have difficulty in distinguishing some spurs from *vegetative shoots*, which do not bear fruit, until you have observed the spurs bursting into blossom.

The *head* is the main framework or branch structure of the tree.

Heading-back, sometimes called *"heading-in"* or just plain *"heading,"* is simply cutting or pruning back parts of the tree.

Laterals are branches. The main branches have laterals, but are laterals themselves in relation to the trunk or main stem of the tree. Taken together, the main limbs or branches form the *scaffold* of the tree.

Leaders are the growths which determine the height and general shape of the tree. A *main leader* type is the typical tree with a single, central trunk. At the other extreme is the *bush* type, with a number of spreading leaders starting near the ground.

A *terminal* refers to a leader shoot as against a lateral shoot. It can also refer to the growing point of any shoot.

PRINCIPLES OF PRUNING

It is important to recognize certain basic pruning principles which are applicable to all tree fruits regardless of degree of dwarfing.

(1) Pruning *is* a dwarfing process. It reduces tree size and thereby dwarfs trees. The fact that pruning often gives rise to localized vigorous shoot growths may give the impression that total tree growth is increased. This, of course, is not true as the total leaf area of a tree is usually reduced in proportion to the severity of pruning.

47

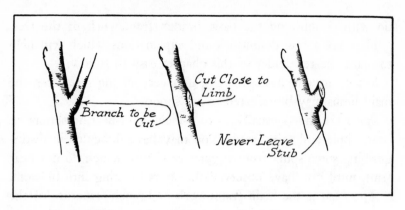

Stubs left in pruning can be very damaging to the tree.

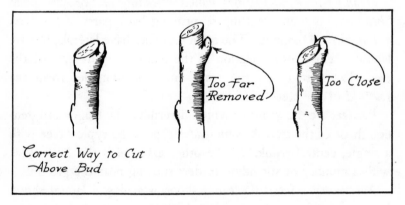

To ensure proper development of a branch, pruning cuts
should be made carefully.

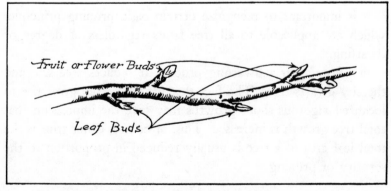

Fruit buds are usually thicker and rounder than leaf buds.

(2) Severe pruning at planting time does not upset a tree nearly so much as similar pruning of an established orchard tree. In digging up a young tree from the nursery much of its root system is damaged; top pruning is usually required to prevent severe set back or even death of the tree due to the lack of balance between the root system and the top. Therefore, it is desirable to prune at planting time. (Some nurseries will do this before shipping, if requested.)

(3) Excessive pruning of young trees may delay blossoming and fruiting. Long succulent shoots fostered by pruning grow late in the season and thus fail to allow manufactured food to accumulate sufficiently to aid in fruit-bud formation. In short, trees can be kept in a juvenile or non-fruiting condition by excessively heavy pruning.

(4) Pruning is a necessary orchard practice. In fact, if no pruning is done, a tree will even attempt to prune itself. Due to natural crowding and shading, limbs will die. This certainly is not a desirable procedure from an orchard management standpoint. Usually, wood is never allowed to become weak and die in well-managed orchards. In a good pruning program, the weak wood which produces the low-grade fruit is cut out whenever found. Weak wood is characteristically thin or small in diameter and often grows downward.

(5) Pruning usually does not alter the natural habit of a plant. A spreading variety like the Rhode Island Greening Apple cannot be made to grow upright like Early McIntosh, or *vice versa*. In pruning, we simply attempt to correct faults and the natural form of the variety is maintained. It is only rarely that we wish to alter drastically the natural form of fruit trees, *i.e.*, in growing espaliers.

(6) Pruning in winter while the trees are dormant is usually preferable to summer pruning. The best time to prune during the dormant season is late winter or early spring—after the danger of severe weather is past. There have been cases of considerable

injury to trees following pruning in the fall or early winter. No pruning should be done while wood is in a frozen condition.

(7) Only *sharp* pruning tools (knife, shears, saw) should be

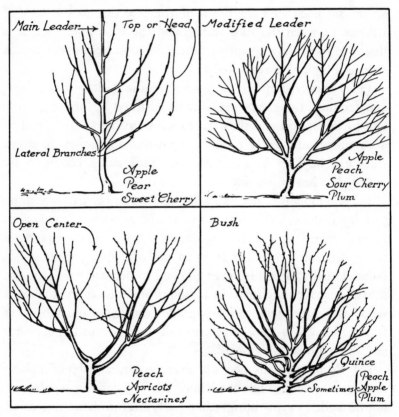

These are the forms to which fruit trees grow, either naturally or by pruning.

used to facilitate the job and to cause as little injury to remaining tissues as possible.

PRUNING THE APPLE AND PEAR

Dwarf apple and pear trees are usually at least two years old and well-branched when sold by nurserymen. For the little tree the lower branches should be about 10 to 18 inches from the ground. With the apple grown as a bush, the head may be started practically at the ground. It is important to keep in mind that the head of a tree does not grow higher from the ground as the tree grows older. A branch one foot from the ground on a small tree will remain at that height if the tree lives one hundred years. In fact, as it increases in diameter the lower side actually will be nearer the ground.

PRUNING AT PLANTING TIME

Try to secure well-grown and nicely branched trees; then set them out in early spring (in some cases late fall planting is practiced) and prune lightly if this has not been done by the nursery. Lightly pruned trees will often produce fruit before those pruned more severely. By light pruning is meant the removal of only those limbs and twigs which seem to be superfluous. If two branches are close together and especially if they are parallel —growing in the same direction—one should be cut out. If the head is too thick some of the competing branches should be removed. In thus selecting the permanent scaffold system, well-distributed branches are chosen so that the tree will not be one-sided. Most small shoots and twigs should be left to help nourish the tree. If a main side branch is abnormally large it is a good practice to head it back to an outward growing lateral and to cut off some of its other laterals. This pruning will tend to dwarf the branch and bring its growth and size into conformity with the rest of the tree. Follow-up pruning will usually be required during the next dormant season because an over-vigorous branch is difficult to keep down.

If a nursery tree has a poorly developed head or if the head is too high (see pages 50 and 52), more severe pruning may be required. In such cases it is suggested that the tree be headed back severely—to 24 inches or less—and that most of the branches be removed at planting. This severe pruning will result in the

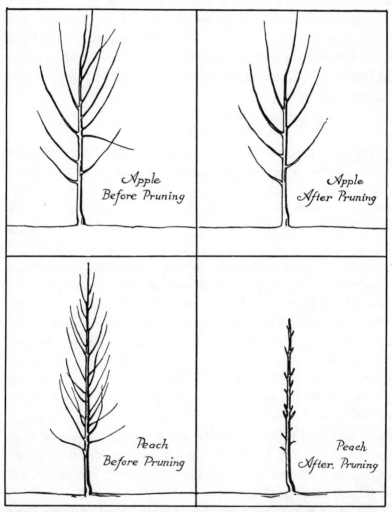

Apple
Before Pruning

Apple
After Pruning

Peach
Before Pruning

Peach
After. Pruning

With dwarf apples, at planting, it is usually sufficient to reduce the number of branches. With peaches and others, more drastic pruning is usually employed.

growth of several branches (shoots) during the first growing season which will allow for branch selection. A well-shaped little tree should result from such a program.

One-year-old unbranched apple and pear trees (whips) may also be bought. These may be planted in the spring and immediately cut back to about 10 inches (above the bud). Subsequent pruning is similar to that described above. Sometimes whips are left unpruned at planting and grow into well-shaped dwarf trees, provided laterals develop properly and low enough down on the trunk.

The pruning treatment at planting is important but it is not the most significant factor in developing good orchard trees. *Good growth, in type and amount, is fundamental.* Pruning the newly-set tree can be helpful in assuring such growth. Obviously, there is no single best way to prune trees. No amount of general or even detailed advice can take the place of *good judgment* since each tree must receive individual treatment.

LATER PRUNING

With well-branched and low-headed dwarf apple and pear trees, further development of the top is not particularly difficult since the trees are allowed to grow almost naturally. A general program of cutting back apple or pear shoots is not recommended. The principal dormant pruning required consists of cutting out suckers and watersprouts, thinning out superfluous branches and suppressing overvigorous shoot growths by cutting them back considerably and consistently. Suckers, as we learned earlier, are shoots, often vigorous, originating from the roots or rootstock. Watersprouts are similar in growth habit, but originate higher up on the tree on the trunk or branches. Both suckers and watersprouts are usually undesirable. A worthwhile point to remember in cutting out these growths is that the cuts be made flush with the parent limb to discourage further suckering from the same area. Never leave stubs. A good way to lessen the

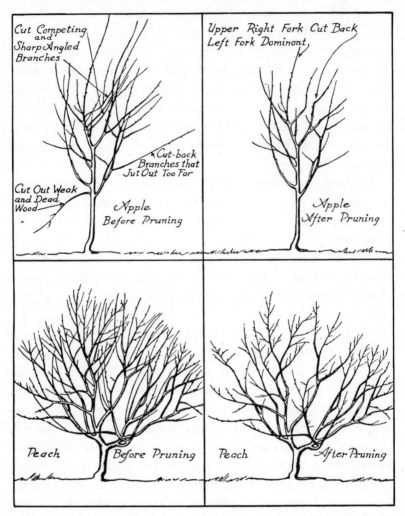

Basic principles of pruning after trees have been set out in the family orchard for a year or more are illustrated. With apples the pruning is primarily to correct faults; with peaches, regular thinning and some cutting back are essential.

54

trouble of these growths is to rub them off during the summer when they are just starting to grow. At this succulent stage, they can be rubbed or pulled off very easily.

Summer pruning is not usually done, except for early removal of suckers and watersprouts and for checking excessive shoot elongation. Shoots growing more than 15 to 20 inches without lateral development may lead to more or less barren stretches of wood—that is, fruit spur development is inhibited. By pinching back the strong-growing vegetative shoots on young trees in early summer, spurring and blossoming are often fostered and more productive trees result. This practice of pinching back or cutting back shoots in summer to cause flower buds to form on them is generally utilized by growers of dwarf trees in Europe.

Occasionally, timely summer pruning is needed to keep a tree growing symmetrically. This means that one or two branches should not be allowed to grow excessively in comparison with the others; they should be pinched or pruned back. Often it is difficult to suppress naturally vigorous portions of a tree, but such growths, often the result of faulty previous pruning, can usually be adjusted if handled correctly. If a limb or branch is becoming too large, it should be winter-pruned more severely than the others and thereby dwarfed. The removal of laterals which are often abundant on strong limbs is often a better way to dwarf a branch than merely heading it back. Since laterals or side branches nourish the main limb, their removal tends to dwarf that limb. A branch is like an army in that if several units are destroyed, the possible growth or "drive" is seriously diminished.

With the little tree and bush type of dwarf tree, it is perhaps as easy to overprune as to prune too little. Summer pruning in particular can easily be overdone. But in moderation, as we have shown, even summer pruning can be used to advantage in checking rampant growth and thereby fostering fruit-bud formation. However, the main stress should be laid on winter pruning. As trees grow older, somewhat more severe pruning is required to maintain vigorous growth and continuous good fruit production year after year.

Annual pruning is very much to be preferred to pruning every two or three years. Only small dormant pruning cuts are usually required. Large cuts and the removal of main limbs foster undue development of undesirable suckers and watersprouts as the tree balance is upset. Numerous, small, thinning-out cuts, on the other hand, result in a general, healthy invigoration which is desirable. The tops should be kept reasonably open through the removal of superfluous branches, and the limbs that interfere with one another should be thinned out.

STAKING

Many dwarf fruit trees trained as bushes or little trees do not require artificial support that is so integral a part of trellis-trained forms. *However, with apples on the Malling IX rootstock and with many dwarf pears staking is usually required.* This is due to the characteristically small growth and poor anchorage of certain dwarfing stocks. Sections of iron pipe or stout wooden stakes set fairly close to each tree and deeply enough to be rigid are suggested. A single tie with a good grade of clothesline approximately 2 to 3 feet above the ground is often adequate for newly planted trees. However, a bearing tree should be tied to the post at two or more points to give rigidity. Cocoanut fiber twine, clothesline, willow wands or heavy galvanized wire may be used for tying. Three precautions should be observed. Whatever tying material is used—and this is particularly important for wire—it should be buffered by means of old garden hose or sacking where it encircles the tree in order to avoid injury to the tender bark. Secondly, in making ties be sure to provide allowance for trunk growth; otherwise girdling of the bark may result. Lastly, clothesline, twine or similar ties should be examined frequently to see if they need to be replaced. Some materials should be replaced each year; wire, of course, is more permanent.

PRUNING QUINCES

Quinces need much less pruning than apples. Very little pruning is done at planting time and only light thinning out of branches is all that is usually required later on. Quinces are grown as bushes or are trained to a low spreading head.

PRUNING THE PEACH AND NECTARINE

Most nursery trees of peach and nectarine are sold at one year of age. After planting, it is usually best to cut off all branches and to cut back the tree to about 24 inches above ground. This allows for a low-headed tree. In the spring of the following year, select four to six branches about equal in size, uniformly distributed around the trunk and having fairly wide crotch angles. Remove all other sizable main branches as well as sharp-angled laterals on the four or six chosen scaffold branches. With peaches as with other fruit trees, narrow crotches are very likely to result in breakage in later years. Sometimes good results will follow the selection of scaffold branches at planting time, but usually good branches are not available on the year-old nursery tree.

After a second summer's growth, it is time to continue the building of the main branch framework of the tree. During the winter select three or four strong side shoots—laterals—which are well spaced along each of the main scaffold branches chosen the previous year. Cut out some of the remaining shoots and cut back those that are left. This will give the few selected side shoots a good chance to develop properly and the result will be a well-shaped tree.

It is usually best to train the peach tree to an open head or vase form since it has a natural inclination to grow this way and hence little alteration of the natural bent is required. As the tree grows older, light heading back of main branches together with thinning out of excess laterals keeps the tree vigorous and fruit-ful. The shoots in the center of the tree should not be removed until the tree is four years of age or older since a large percentage of the first crops may be borne on these shoots. Later on it is best to keep the inside shaded portions of the tree fairly well pruned out since the bearing area soon shifts to the periphery or outer circumference of the tree.

With peach and nectarine trees, more drastic pruning is often needed than with the other fruits, particularly apples and pears. This is due to the fact that instead of producing fruit on long-lived spurs, the peach fruits only on shoot wood that grew the previous summer. Annual pruning to get rid of old wood and to invigorate productive new growth is thus essential. The significance of proper pruning here is too often underestimated. Shearing the tops of bearing peach trees at a definite height is not necessary. In comparison with moderate thinning out of branches and laterals, this drastic heading practice delays bearing, reduces yield, and gives a dense top which is difficult to spray or dust. However, sufficient wood should be cut out each year to avoid overcrowding, to control tree size and to keep the fruiting wood within reach. This does mean heavy pruning when compared to apples.

PRUNING THE CHERRY, PLUM AND APRICOT

Of the various orchard fruits, sweet cherry trees are usually pruned the least. When planting a two-year-old tree in early spring, about four main branches should be selected for the main framework and all others removed. If the branches are not too long—24 inches—and if the tips are in good condition, cutting back will not be necessary. Otherwise, they may be shortened to 20 to 24 inches. The central leader is usually cut back only slightly. During the ensuing two or three years, several additional framework branches can be selected and the leader suppressed by cutting it back to an outward growing branch. Young

Some orchardists use traps to monitor the presence of coddling moths on their dwarf apple trees, to determine when to spray.

sweet cherry trees tend to grow upright and to branch sparingly. Cutting back of long shoots to outward-growing buds in the spring before growth starts will tend to invigorate lower branching and to cause a broader head. A modified leader tree (see page 50) with well-spaced branches is desirable. Sometimes one-year-old trees or whips are set out and do exceedingly well. These are usually cut back at planting time to 25 to 30 inches and subsequent head development proceeds as above described.

Thus, the pruning required during the first four years consists of light thinning out, light heading back to outside buds or branches to encourage a spreading-out habit of growth and the removal of interfering limbs. Older bearing trees need very little pruning. The crop is formed laterally on spurs and since sweet cherry trees branch very little as they grow older, it is unnecessary and unwise to do much thinning out. Some cutting back of old trees will cause invigoration and new spur development but should be done with caution.

The sour cherry is a naturally spreading tree which requires comparatively little pruning. Although some growers practice annual cutting back to increase vigor, thinning-out type of pruning, to eliminate crowding branches, is suggested for the home gardener. The modified leader system is desirable, as for sweet cherries.

When planting sour cherry trees it is best to thin out the branches moderately, leaving the leader in the dominant position; cutting back the scaffold branches to 20 inches is often done but this is usually not necessary. The lowest branch may be left about 12 inches above the ground. During the next three years, further selection of framework branches can be made. As the tree grows older, it may respond quite well to moderate pruning such as thinning out the tops. This helps to keep the tree in good vigor and aids in keeping the inside spurs and lower fruiting wood productive. This annual pruning also tends to increase terminal and lateral growth and hence fosters the development of a large, healthy spur system.

Plum trees require very little pruning while young. When two-year-old trees are planted, it is customary to select about four of the most vigorous and best-spaced branches for the main framework or head. These branches need not be headed back provided they are not excessively long. Other competing branches are removed and further training is similar to that described for the sweet cherry. In general, Japanese varieties need heavier pruning than the others to obtain good tree shape and sufficiently vigorous growth of shoots. Thinning out of slender branches is especially important with such a variety as Burbank.

As plum trees grow older, more severe pruning is necessary, particularly with the Japanese sorts. It is usually important to head back both terminals and laterals and to keep the tops well thinned out.

The Domestica plums which comprise the majority of the varieties suggested for the home gardener require only a light thinning out type of pruning. This difference in pruning needs between the two types of plums is worth noting.

The apricot is pruned in much the same way as the Japanese plum, but somewhat more severely since the fruit spurs are shorter-lived. Annual cutting back of shoots and thinning out of crowded branches result in good spur development and vigorous productive trees.

PRUNING WOUNDS

Whenever a branch is cut off, a wound results. Wounds on healthy trees usually heal over in a year or two as a result of callus-growth. Over this callus, new cambium eventually develops and forms normal bark and sapwood so that the dead wood of the wound is covered with living tissue. The faster a wound heals, the less opportunity there is for rot-causing organisms to become established in the exposed heartwood. Stubs heal slowly if at all; therefore all cuts should be made "flush" or as close to the parent limb as possible. Large wounds naturally heal more slowly than small ones. On healthy vigorous trees, wounds up to 2 inches in diameter will usually heal over quickly enough to prevent rotting of the exposed wood.

In some cases, certain asphalt preparations such as "Tree Seal" are useful in coating the larger tree wounds. In tests made by the United States Department of Agriculture, common shellac was one of the best wound dressings tried. On the other hand, many materials and commercial preparations have been found to be more harmful than beneficial, and for this reason, home gardeners should take due precautions before using wound coverings on their trees. Avoid drastic pruning and large cuts by pruning each year.

SUMMARY

Some pruning manuals go into more precise details in directions for pruning the different tree fruits. Almost invariably, it is impossible to follow such directions. Each tree is individualistic and is different in few or many respects from every other tree. Each tree thus requires individual attention and treatment. Pruning cannot be standardized. It is well worth while to repeat that no carefully worded directions can take the place of judgment and good sense in the pruning of fruit trees.

As long as a few main ideas are kept in mind, pruning fruit trees should not be particularly difficult.

(1) Pruning is the removal of a part or parts of a tree.

(2) It is a useful practice in aiding trees to become established at planting time, in training trees to desirable forms, in inducing vigor, in ridding trees of excess, decadent and other undesirable parts and in helping the production of annual crops of high quality fruit.

(3) Trees are pruned when planted to compensate for the reduced root system (as a result of digging).

(4) Young trees are pruned to train them to desirable forms and to obtain a good branch framework.

(5) Bearing trees are pruned to thin out thick and weakened wood and to foster vigor and continued fruitfulness.

(6) As trees grow older, the need for pruning increases.

(7) It usually is better to prune lightly to moderately since excessive pruning is counter-productive.

Proud exhibitor of a nicely shaped dwarf apple tree.

8

Thin for Bigger Fruit

In order to get bigger fruit and improve the quality it is often necessary to do some *thinning*. This simply means picking some of the excess fruit before it is allowed to develop very much. Fruit trees in general tend to produce more fruit than they can nurture. If some of the excess is not picked off, the tree will produce a great deal of undersized fruit of rather poor quality. It is much like thinning carrots in your garden and is done for the same reason.

With dwarf trees, thinning is especially important because they have a strong tendency to produce too much fruit. If you do not thin your dwarf trees you will probably get small fruits of poor quality and color. Also some of the branches may become overladen and break off.

Overproduction in any *one* year may bring about the undesirable biennial bearing tendency where blossoming and fruiting occur every other year instead of annually. Furthermore, too heavy cropping sometimes brings about lowered vitality and increases the chance for winter injury. Thus there are sound reasons for thinning other than the more obvious one of producing better and larger fruits.

We recommend this easy way to do your thinning:

(1) About six weeks after blossoming, when the young fruit is beginning to size, pick off the undersized, diseased, wormy, or deformed specimens.

(2) Then pick off all the fruits necessary to leave the allowed number which is given in the table below for each kind of fruit.

Result of failure to thin. Bough has broken from weight of fruit.

The technique of thinning is simple, but you will find it easier to use a slightly different technique for different fruits as follows:

Thinning apples, pears and plums: You should pick the fruit without removing the stem from the branch. Grasp the fruit with the thumb and forefinger and push it away from the stem with the other fingers. This puts the entire strain on the stem, leaving it attached to the tree and eliminating damage to the spurs.

You should learn to recognize a *spur*. This is a short stubby shoot growing directly out of the branch and bearing fruit. See

Unthinned   *Thinned*

A comparative test in a university orchard shows the benefits of thinning fruit. Not only are the apples at right larger, but they are of a deeper and more even color. Danger of breaking trunks or limbs is lessened.

page 47, also at blossom time note which growths carry the blossoms. Many apple and pear spurs bear fruit every other year.

Thinning peaches, nectarines and apricots: Grasp the fruit and twist it from the stem.

Fruit-Thinning Table

Apples	Leave 1 fruit every 6–8 inches and
Pears	usually leave only 1 fruit per spur.
Peaches	
Nectarines	Leave 1 fruit every 6–8 inches.
Plums	Leave 1 fruit every 3–4 inches.
Cherries	
Quince	Thinning usually not necessary.

9

Soil Management and Fertilization

The soil in which trees are planted is very important. It serves as an anchorage for the trees as well as for the ground cover; it is a storehouse for some of the basic materials from which the plant makes food; it literally teems with soil micro-organisms that make crude plant food materials available for plant growth; and it is a reservoir of water, a steady and adequate supply of which is vital to good growth and fruitfulness. The ideal soil is deep, well-drained yet retentive of moisture and capable of supplying essential plant food materials. Through soil management practices such as drainage, the addition of organic matter, liming, fertilization, and cultivation, most soils can be made to provide the requirements for good growth of fruit trees. This is significant since the home gardener usually must make the best of the situation as he finds it; in most instances it is not possible, nor necessary for good success with dwarf fruit trees to have an ideal soil situation to start with.

Except in early spring, water should not stand for any length of time on soil planted to fruit trees. If a home-owner is faced with this situation, the possibility of drainage, either ditch or tile, should be considered. Fruit trees cannot stand "wet feet" for long periods. On the other hand, a soil site for the proposed dwarf orchard may be sandy and excessively drained. The addition of organic matter in the form of organic manures, green manure crops or surface mulches may be the answer. In other

Chickens foraging in a small homestead orchard help to control the insects which might be harmful to the dwarf fruit trees.

68

cases, where a heavy, established sod interferes with good tree growth, cultivation or possibly mulching may be utilized to alleviate the situation. In short, though the home gardener will rarely be blessed with ideal soil conditions, he can make much progress in the direction of that ideal by good management practices over a period of years. With dwarf fruit trees in particular, the returns from sound soil management are well worth achieving. *It should be emphasized that dwarf fruit culture requires a relatively high condition of nutrition for best results.*

SOIL NUTRIENTS

Soil fertility is the crop-producing power of the soil and is largely dependent on the supply of available plant food. Fruit

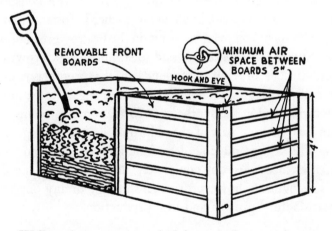

Well made compost worked in around a tree is very beneficial. In the compost box shown above, vegetable wastes and crop residues are mixed in the left section with manure, soil and lime or wood ashes. After six weeks the partly decomposed material is turned over into the right section for six weeks of "ripening."

trees normally take from the soil the following elements: nitrogen, phosphorus, sulfur, potassium, calcium, and magnesium in considerable quantities; smaller amounts of iron, manganese, sodium, chlorine and silicon; and very small quantities of "trace" elements such as copper, zinc, boron, etc. In addition, of course, all green plants utilize hydrogen and oxygen in the form of water absorbed by the roots and carbon obtained as carbon dioxide from the air.

Of the elements of plant food furnished fruit trees by the soil, only a few are apt to become deficient enough to require replenishment under normal conditions. These are nitrogen, phosphorus and potassium. In addition, magnesium, calcium, boron and zinc have had to be supplied in a number of cases in recent years. Each element has a separate function to perform in the development of a plant; hence, if any one is present in insufficient amount, deficiency symptoms become evident followed by poor growth and fruiting. Nitrogen is a constituent of protein and is present in all living tissue; it fosters stem and leaf development and helps to maintain the healthy green of well-nourished trees; phosphorus is said to stimulate root growth and is a constituent of vital compounds in the protoplasm of the living cells; potassium is supposed to aid in sugar formation and translocation and in the synthesis or formation of proteins; magnesium is an integral part of the chlorophyll or green pigment in leaves. The exact and complete functions of these and other essential elements are not completely understood; the need for each is recognized, however, since a shortage of any one results in unsatisfactory growth and low production.

ORGANIC MATTER

Soil organic matter originates from plants, animals and microbes and is a very important constituent of the soil. It includes the partially decomposed matter commonly known as humus. Organic matter is a storehouse of plant nutrients, increases water-holding capacity, promotes better aeration, and, in general, makes the soil a more favorable medium for the development of plant root systems. Sources of organic matter include animal manures,

Buckwheat planted as a cover crop in a dwarf fruit orchard.

green plants, hay, straw, seaweed, sawdust, lawn clippings, peat moss, etc.

Specially prepared compost or synthetic manure can be made from materials such as straw, old or spoiled hay, leaves, garden refuse, etc. A compost pile is built up out-of-doors as these materials become available. Small amounts of a nitrogen fertilizer, limestone, and superphosphate are added as the pile is gradually built up. The compost pile is watered and turned three or four times at monthly intervals. The resulting compost material is as beneficial to growing plants as the average well-rotted manure.

CULTIVATION AND MULCHING

Dwarf fruit trees respond splendidly to wise cultural methods. During the first year or so following planting, cultivation of the entire area may well be practiced to give the trees a good start, provided of course that soil erosion—more serious on sloping land—is not a factor. Cultivation destroys competing grass and weed growth and releases nitrogen and mineral food elements from the soil organic matter. In any case, a circular area at least 4 feet in diameter around each tree should be kept free of weeds. Mulching this area to a depth of 2 to 6 inches with lawn clippings, granulated peat moss, hay, straw or sawdust is an excellent practice. This organic material insulates the soil against wide temperature changes, lessens heaving damage due to alternate freezing and thawing of the soil surface, maintains an even moisture supply and provides fertility. *Surface mulching is very effective in making the productive top inches of the soil a better feeding area for tree roots.* It also entices mice, so leave a space free of mulch for several inches around the tree trunks; if there are signs that the rodents are gnawing the trunks, lay poisons for them, or protect trunks with hardware cloth.

Dwarf trees may also be grown successfully in a clipped lawn with only the area adjacent to the trunk kept cultivated or mulched.

Firm staking with ties is best. A section of metal pipe is neater and more lasting than wood.

Well-rotted manure and good compost material are unsur-passed as fertilizers for dwarf fruit trees. A pound or two per square foot, about twelve pounds to a tree, or in the gardener's terminology—"a reasonably good coating" of animal manure is a commonly suggested rate of application. If dried manures are used, the amounts needed—in pounds—are less. Suggested dressings of dried manures are: cow, 2½ pounds per tree; horse, 2 pounds; sheep, 1½; poultry, 1. Applications are best made in the spring, and should be spread over an area somewhat beyond the reach of the branches and in no case closer than one foot from the trunk.

Commercial fertilizers can be used satisfactorily provided good judgment is exercised. Excessive dosages must be avoided. Probably a mixed or so-called "complete" garden fertilizer containing nitrogen, phosphoric acid and potash is the most logical choice. For instance a 5–10–5 (5% nitrogen, 10% phosphoric acid, 5% potash) or 5–8–7 formula may be used at the rate of perhaps ¼ pound per tree. Apply it in the spring around each tree under and just beyond the spread of the branches and no closer than one foot from the trunk. In order to supply enough nitrogen, additional use of a nitrogen fertilizer such as nitrate of soda is often required, particularly for older trees. One-quarter pound per tree is a good dressing. The older the dwarf tree, the greater the need for fertilizer. This increased need is due not only to heavier crops of fruit, but also to the fact that the roots of older trees have rather thoroughly exploited the soil. Overnitrating as evidenced by excessive vegetative growth is possible and should be avoided. In some cases, soils may be rich enough to require only very moderate amounts of fertilizer; in other cases, more dependence will need to be placed on annual fertilizer additions.

In many home orchard locations the soil is naturally acid and may need lime. A soil testing service to determine acidity and

Second-year dwarf apple, peach and pear trees planted in the lawn area of a country home, extensive vegetable gardens behind.

the consequent need for lime is available at many state colleges. A good soil pH reading for fruit trees is from 5.5 to 6.5. It is suggested that a finely pulverized, high magnesium limestone be applied at the rate of approximately 10 pounds per hundred square feet. If possible, this lime should be dug into the soil as much as possible because, unlike nitrate of soda, it penetrates the soil very slowly. A high magnesium lime is recommended because it has recently been found that many soils, particularly in the Atlantic coastal states, are deficient in magnesium. One application of lime every four or five years should usually be sufficient.

In every case, the amounts of organic and/or inorganic fertilizers to use in dwarf fruit tree culture should be determined not entirely on theoretical grounds but also on actual need as portrayed by tree performance—vegetative growth and fruit production. If a tree is performing satisfactorily, there is little excuse for drastically altering the fertilizer program. If growth is inadequate, applications may be increased and vice versa. There is no single right way to grow dwarf trees—except to grow them well. Soil fertilization is a means to that end.

The apples are ripe, so don't shake the tree!

10

Program for Pest Control

As we brought out in an earlier chapter, pests in great variety and of extreme durability have always made things difficult for fruit-growers. Programs of rather formidable intricacy have had to be worked out for pest control on a commercial scale.

Fortunately for the home fruit grower, a good deal of simplification is possible. For one thing, the planting of dwarf trees in itself makes control easier, because with the help of convenient sprayers every part of a tree can be reached in a minute or two. For another, there are new and more effective control materials available. Often, it is feasible to apply to the orchard the same spray with which the home-owner makes war on bugs and blights in his garden.

Today, the home grower with small to medium-sized trees can avoid the complications of commercial practice and still, with a minimum of work, produce a high percentage of good, sound, luscious tree-fruits.

The one fundamental that needs to be kept in mind is that all pests may be classified as either insects or diseases. Some controls are effective on insects, others on diseases. A combination of these controls will give an all-purpose spray which in most cases will be sufficiently effective for the home orchardist.

INSECTS AND INSECTICIDES

Fruit tree insects vary in life history, method of attack and vulnerability to insecticides. Some are chewers like beetles, bor-

APPLE SCAB—on fruit and leaf.

TENT CATERPILLAR—nest and worm.

PLUM CURCULIO— egg, adult beetle, larva in young fruit.

CODLING MOTH— and larva in apple.

APPLE MAGGOT— maggot tunnels in apple and adult fly.

APHID—newly hatched lice on bud, distorted fruit and leaf.

ORIENTAL FRUIT— MOTH—wilting tip and larva.

SAN JOSE SCALE— and young crawler.

OYSTERSHELL SCALE—enlarged female and crawlers.

EUROPEAN RED MITE—leaf injury and over-wintering eggs.

PEACH BORER— moth, borer and jelly-like frass at trunk base.

BLACK KNOT DISEASE—on plum branch.

ers and caterpillers and attack foliage and fruit. Stomach poisons or contact insecticides are used to combat them. Others such as aphids (plant lice) and mites are of the sucking type. They are killed with contact or fumigant insecticides. These are some of the better insecticides available:

KELTHANE (DICOFOL)—to control European red mite and spider mites.
MALATHION—to control aphids, mites and scale insects in the crawler stage.
METHOXYCHLOR—to control codling moth, oriental fruit moth, curculio and Japanese beetle (replaces DDT).
SEVIN (CARBARYL)—to control Japanese beetle and apple maggot.
THIODAN (ENDOSULFAN)—to control peach tree borers.

DISEASES AND CONTROL MATERIALS

Diseases of fruit trees are usually fungal or bacterial in nature. Of these, the most common are the fungus troubles such as scab, brown rot and rusts. A bacterial disease is fire blight, most prevalent on pear trees. Some of the favored fungicides are the following:

CAPTAN—a yellow powder to control apple scab, peach brown rot and other fungus diseases of fruit trees and brambles (but not effective on powdery mildew).
CYPREX (DODINE)—for control of apple scab primarily.
DIKAR—fungicide—miticide containing dithane and karathane for control of scab, rusts, powdery mildew and mites.
FERBAM (FERMATE, COROMATE, etc.)—for control of leaf spots, apple rust and black rot of grapes.
KARATHANE—a yellow powder specific for control of powdery mildew on fruit trees and ornamentals.
WETTABLE SULFUR—old line fungicide for control of fungus diseases.
ZINEB (DITHANE, PARZATE, etc.)—white powder for control of sooty blotch, apple rust, etc.

SPRAY EQUIPMENT

Various types of sprayers are available at hardware stores, garden supply centers and spray equipment dealers. The compressed air sprayer has a 2 to 4 gallon cylindrical tank with a hand operated air pump. The knapsack sprayer usually has a 4 gallon tank carried on the back and is equipped with a hand operated single or double action pump. The hand spray gun or so called trombone sprayer has a double action slide pump and hose, one end of which is placed in a bucket of liquid spray material. Small power driven sprayers are also available.

Another convenient type of spray equipment for fruit trees is the garden hose or proportioner sprayer. The pressure is derived from the home water system. The desired spray chemicals are mixed in water. The container with the proportioning device and nozzle is attached to a garden hose. When the container is emptied shut off the water and replenish the spray mixture. These "hose-on" applicators are easy to use. Just follow directions that come with the equipment.

With any sprayer, the manufacturer's instructions should be followed. Also, a sprayer should be cleaned out after each spraying since even small amounts of spray material left in the pump or spray nozzle may clog and corrode the parts.

GENERAL PURPOSE SPRAY

A recommended general purpose spray formula utilizes three materials: captan, malathion and methoxychlor. The table gives amounts of commercial products for three quantities of spray, i.e., 2, 5 and 25 gallons. This is a general spray that is effective against many troublesome insects and diseases. This mixture can be purchased ready-mixed from garden supply stores, or the three ingredients can be purchased separately and mixed as in the table. If you use a commercially prepared mixture, it is suggested that the label directions be followed carefully.

Sulfur, Zineb, Kelthane and Sevin are used for special purposes to beef up the general purpose mixture. Note the rates of each and their specific uses in the table "Special Purpose Sprays."

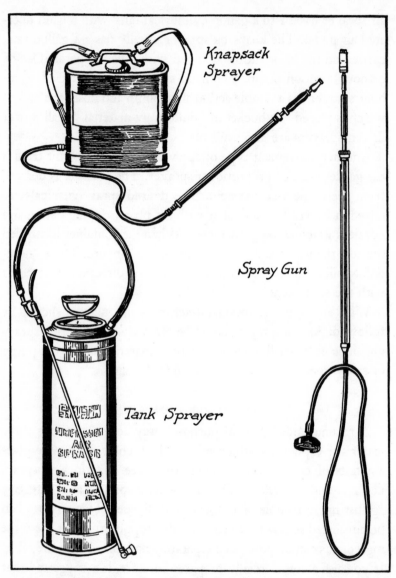

Knapsack Sprayer

Spray Gun

Tank Sprayer

These are useful sprayers for orchard and garden use on a small scale. The compressed air sprayer is "pumped-up," and spray released as needed. The spray gun is used with a pail or barrel; the solution is sucked up and sprayed by a back-and-forth movement of the device on the hose. The knapsack sprayer works on the same principle but is handier to transport.

GENERAL PURPOSE SPRAY MIXTURE

Material	2 gallons	5 gallons	25 gallons
Captan 50% Wettable Powder or Cyprex 65% Wettable Powder	3 tablespoons	1/2 cup	1/2 lb
Malathion 25% Wettable Powder	6 tablespoons	2/3 cup	3/4 lb
Methoxychlor 50% Wettable Powder	6 tablespoons	2/3 cup	3/4 lb

SPECIAL PURPOSE SPRAYS

Material	2 gallons	5 gallons	25 gallons
Wettable Sulfur*	4 tablespoons	1/2 cup	1 lb
Zineb 65% Wettable Powder**	2 tablespoons	1/4 cup	1/4 lb
Kelthane AP Wettable Powder***	3 tablespoons	1/2 cup	1/2 lb
Sevin 50W Wettable Powder****	4 tablespoons	1/2 cup	1 lb

* Necessary for control of powdery mildew. Apply in prebloom and petal-fall sprays. Do not use on grapes.
** For control of sooty blotch of apple.
*** For mite control. Apply about 20 and 40 days after petal fall.
**** For apple maggot, one spray about June 20, the second about July 5, the third about July 20.

A question may be raised concerning dusting. There are available one-package general purpose dust mixtures and these are quite easy to use in hand dusting equipment. However, experience has shown that dusting is less effective than spraying and the nuisance of dust blowing around in a neighborhood counteracts the favorable features. If a dust is used, be sure to follow label directions and be sure to get complete coverage of the trees. More applications will be needed than with sprays for equivalent disease and insect control.

A SPRAY SCHEDULE consists of several specific sprays to accomplish over-all control of insect and disease problems over the entire season from start of spring growth, through blossoming, to fruit harvest. Considerable dependence is placed on the general purpose mixture with specific additions to accomplish improved control of specific pests. Two schedules are given here, one for the pome fruits (apples, pears, quince), one for the stone fruits (peach, cherry, plum). Note that for best overall pest control, some ten spray applications are needed. In some situations certain of the applications may be omitted if one wants to "take a chance." However, it is best to follow the *schedule*.

APPLE, PEAR, QUINCE SPRAY SCHEDULE

Time of Application	Materials for 5 Gallons Water	To Control
DELAYED DORMANT leaves 1/2-3/4 inch	general purpose mixture plus wettable sulfur 1/2 cup	scab, leaf spots, mildew
PREPINK when blossom buds show pink	same as above	scab, leaf spots, mildew, aphids
PINK just before bloom	same as above	scab, leaf spots, mildew, aphids
BLOOM	Captan 1/2 cup sulfur 1/2 cup	scab, mildew
PETAL FALL	same as Delayed Dormant	scab, mildew, aphids, other insects
FIRST COVER TO SIXTH COVER (begin 10 days after petal fall and repeat at 10-14 day intervals for six applications)	general purpose mixture plus Zineb 1/4 cup	scab, blotch, insects
	add Kelthane 1/2 cup in second and fourth covers	mites
	add Sevin 1/2 cup beginning June 20 for three applications	apple maggot

PEACH, CHERRY, PLUM SPRAY SCHEDULE

Time of Application	Materials for 5 Gallons Water	To Control
DORMANT before buds begin to swell	Ferbam 3/4 cup	peach leaf curl
BLOSSOM SPRAYS apply just before and during bloom	general purpose mixture	blossom blight, plant bugs, curculio
PETAL FALL	same as above	brown rot, leaf spots, fruit moth, curculio
8 DAY SPRAY 8 days after petal fall	same as above	brown rot, leaf spots, fruit moth, curculio
FIRST COVER TO FIFTH COVER (Begin 10 days after 8-day spray and repeat at 10-14 day intervals for five applications)	same as above add Sevin 1/2 cup for Japanese beetle	brown rot, scab, curculio, fruit moth, aphid
PREHARVEST (three sprays at 7-10 day intervals beginning a month before harvest)	Captan 1/2 cup	brown rot on fruit

GRAPE SPRAY SCHEDULE

(Although grapes are not considered fruit trees and therefore are not included in this book, this spray schedule is included as a bonus for those having a small vineyard.)

Time of Application	Materials for 5 Gallons Water	To Control
PREBLOOM NO. 1 when shoots are 8-12 inches long	general purpose mixture (no sulfur)	black rot, flea beetle

Time of Application	Materials for 5 Gallons Water	To Control
PREBLOOM NO. 2 just before bloom	same as above	black rot, berry moth, leaf hopper, mildew
AFTER BLOOM immediately after bloom	same as above	black rot, berry moth, leaf hopper
10 DAYS LATER	same as above	black rot, berry moth, leaf hopper
PEA SIZE when grapes are pea size	same as above plus 2/3 cup Sevin	black rot, berry moth, Japanese beetle
JUNE-JULY	1/2 cup Sevin	only if needed for Japanese beetle

SPECIAL PROBLEMS

Peach Tree Borer: A severe insect problem of peach, plum and cherry trees is the peach tree borer which must be controlled. If not controlled, the trees suffer from holes made by white grub-like borers in the trunks. The trees put out quantities of gum. Use ⅓ cup Thiodan 50% wettable powder in 5 gallons of water and spray the lower trunks thoroughly with three applications about June 15, July 20 and August 25. This spray is designed to kill newly hatched borers on the bark. With only a few trees, the borers can be dug out with a knife or sharp hook. It is not easy to get all the borers and some injury to the trees results.

Black Knot of Plum and Cherry: Black knot is noticed as hard rough galls on the larger branches, especially on plums. Prune out diseased branches in the fall or early spring and burn the prunings. Spray in delayed dormant stage (buds showing a little green) with Zineb, 1 pound in 50 gallons of water, or ½ cup in

5 gallons. Also, protect new growth with a second spray 10 days after the first one. Usually, well-sprayed trees, as in the program outlined in the peach, cherry, plum spray schedule, are less troubled with black knot than neglected trees.

Fire Blight: This is a bacterial disease which can be especially destructive to pears and quince, and sometimes affects apples, flowering crab, Pyracantha and flowering quince. It can kill blossoms, shoots, branches and entire trees. The disease also produces diseased twigs and canker areas on limbs and trunks. The sudden wilting and dying of new growth in the spring is caused by a bacterium which is spread by rain and insects. Often the blossoms are blighted first, then the leaves and twigs. The dead leaves may hang on all summer.

Do not heavily fertilize pear or quince trees since lush succulent growth is especially susceptible to the disease. Rub off new suckers and water sprouts while very small. Cut out cankers and diseased limbs during the dormant season. Finally, there is an effective spray. Use streptomycin antibiotic sold as Agri-mycin 17 or Agristrep. In 5 gallons of water mix 2 rounded tablespoonfuls of 15% product and apply three sprays beginning at early bloom with two follow-up sprays at 5 day intervals.

Cold Injury to Peaches and Apricots: A failure of peaches and apricots to blossom can be caused by low winter temperatures (below −10° F.). The flower buds are killed. If you live in a locality which usually experiences such low winter temperatures, it may be wise to forego including peaches and nectarines in your fruit tree planting. Some things you can do to help trees to withstand cold injury are these: (1) train young trees carefully, leaving no more than three main scaffold limbs, (2) be careful in using nitrogen fertilizer in late summer or fall since late growth can make a tree more tender to cold, (3) keep your trees growing moderately—neither too lush nor growing poorly, (4) do not allow depressions in the soil around the base of trees which can fill with water and ice, (5) thin the fruit so that the drain on the tree is not too heavy, (6) control borers which are debilitating, (7) in very cold winter locations, don't plant trees in low areas receiving cold air drainage from higher areas.

FINAL ADVICE

1. Adequate and timely spray coverage of entire trees is essential for good pest control. Partial coverage will give partial control. Pest damage occurring from missed or poorly timed sprays often cannot be corrected by other sprays later in the season. The best advice is to follow the schedule.

2. The materials and spray schedules outlined should provide good disease and insect control. On the other hand, spray-chemical manufacturers or marketers may offer somewhat different one-package, general purpose mixtures. These should perform satisfactorily if used in accordance with the label recommendations.

3. With all commercial products, it is vital to follow closely and accurately the manufacturer's use directions and handling precautions. Remember that product labeling is registered by the Environmental Protection Agency (E.P.A.) in Washington, D.C.

4. Handle all pest control products carefully and keep them out of reach of children at all times. Store in closed containers where animals cannot get to them. Keep spray materials and sprays out of eyes. Also, keep spray from skin and clothing. Remember that these materials are somewhat to quite toxic and should be so treated. Read labels in their entirety, follow use directions, and heed caution statements. Do not be careless.

5. Methoxychlor, Ferbam, Zineb, Karathane and Thiodan should not be used closer to harvest than 10 to 30 days. It is good practice to stop making application of any material at least 2 weeks before harvest.

6. Do not hesitate to consult your local county agent or state university specialist for published information or other advice.

Become acquainted with these free services and use them. Your county Extension Agent can supply commercial fruit spray schedules to anyone requesting them. They can also identify pests and problems.

Courtesy Michigan State University

Six-year-old Red Delicious on MM 106, a good semi-dwarfing rootstock. This produces a "man-sized" tree and would fit situations where wider spacing is possible.

11

Harvesting–Best Time to Pick Fruits

A very gratifying feature of growing one's own tree fruits is that each variety can be picked at the best time for maximum eating or keeping quality.

The home orchardist can delay the harvest of peaches, for instance, to obtain that exquisite eating quality associated only with tree-ripened fruit. Large growers and those who must ship to distant markets are forced to pick a part of their crops at a relatively immature stage, and quality is sacrificed. There is really no comparison between some commercially handled, perishable fruits of the peach, apricot, nectarine, plum and sweet cherry and the home-grown product. To a lesser extent, perhaps, home-grown apples, pears, prunes and sour cherries may have higher eating quality than the same varieties bought at the retail counters of the local store. A contributing factor here is the comparative freedom from bruising of home-grown fruits—bruising is a very serious problem in commercial fruit handling and accounts for heavy loss.

The determination of the best time to pick each variety of the different tree fruits is not too easy for the inexperienced home orchardist or amateur fruit grower. However, there are certain rather definite indicators of maturity which should help considerably in this regard. As most fruits ripen, there is a perceptible softening of the flesh which gradually becomes more juicy, sweet and palatable. Starches change to sugars, and the disagreeable tannins characteristic of green or immature fruit tend to disappear. A period of a week or two just before harvest can

Mulch under tree prevents injury to fruit that drops at harvest time.

make all the difference in the world in fruit quality. Furthermore, since most fruits continue to grow as long as they remain attached to the tree, there is a significant increase in total yield as a result of this "final swell" or size increase. Of course it is also important that picking precede natural abscission or fruit dropping. Normally, fruit maturity of most tree fruits is accompanied by definite changes in the abscission zone between the fruit stem and the supporting spur. The cells in this area undergo changes which effectively bring about an actual separation of tissues resulting in natural dropping of the fruit. The weakening of this stem connection is another good indicator of maturity.

In addition to softening of the flesh and ease of separation of the fruit from the tree, there is another important and quite reliable index of maturity, again particularly useful for apples. As most varieties become mature, the ground color, which will show through the red color or blush, changes from a deep green to a lighter shade, and eventually to yellowish. The proper time to pick is when the signs of yellowing begin to appear. However, ground color of fully red blushed fruits, such as the red bud sports, is not readily apparent and hence may not be so useful as an index of maturity.

Pears usually should be harvested in a condition that would seem to the amateur to be quite unripe and immature. However, if allowed to yellow on the tree, pears develop gritty cells in the flesh and fail to ripen up satisfactorily. Pears should be harvested when the dark green of the skin *just begins* to fade to a yellowish green. At this stage, the fruits will begin to separate more readily from the spurs.

Peaches, nectarines, apricots, plums and cherries should be allowed to ripen and mellow on the tree. Fully ripened fruits of these kinds will be truly sweet and juicy and have the most delectable flavor if allowed to develop properly. If picked in an immature condition, as is often done in commercial plantings, the ultimate in quality is usually not attained. Color alone is not an accurate criterion of quality development since attractive skin coloration often precedes considerably the adequate ripening of the flesh. If using fresh, allow the fruits to become almost "dead ripe" before picking and enjoy your crop to the utmost. For canning purposes, of course, less mature fruit is satisfactory and sometimes preferable.

Quinces may be picked more or less at your leisure during the late fall. These fruits usually do not soften perceptibly on the tree and are not used as fresh fruit. For processing into jelly or preserves, the actual date of harvest is not particularly significant.

PRE-HARVEST DROP PROBLEM

With certain apple varieties such as McIntosh, a tendency to early pre-harvest dropping is present with a resultant loss of fruit quality due to lack of color and bruising. There are two methods of reducing losses due to pre-harvest dropping of fruit. With dwarf fruit trees in particular, the use of a hay mulch under the trees in the fall will greatly lessen the bruising damage to fruits that drop off prior to picking. Materials other than hay may be used, the main consideration being that the material have a certain amount of "give" to absorb or cushion the impact of the falling fruit successfully. This is an added attribute of the heavy mulch system of tree fruit culture, as outlined previously. A second means of lessening drop-losses is the use of the recently developed hormone or harvest sprays and dusts. Very dilute sprays or dusts containing a chemical, such as alpha naphthalene acetic acid, have the effect of delaying the natural dropping of many fruits, particularly certain apple and pear varieties. Applications are made a week or so before expected harvest, or as soon as pre-harvest dropping of fruit begins. There are several reasonably priced commercial preparations on the market.

With early varieties of apples, and with many varieties of stone fruits, the period during which picking must be done is often very short—a few days, at the most. Hence, it is very important to follow the development of these sorts very closely.

As the cooler weather of fall comes on, the number of days during which picking can be done is increased. Harvest of late varieties should be completed prior to expected heavy frosts and

A heavily laden branch at harvest time. A higher stake with two ties and thinning of the fruit would have prevented this.

freezing weather. Apples exposed to one or two frosts, or even slight freezes, will not be ruined, provided they are not touched while they thaw out naturally.

12

How to Store Fruits

It is well to emphasize again the necessity of handling fruits without bruising them. This is especially important if fruits are to be stored for any length of time. Only well-grown, disease- and insect-free specimens picked at the right time—well before fully ripe—and handled without bruising are good storage risks. It is usually unprofitable to store poor fruit. Late ripening varieties of apples and pears are the fruits usually stored for winter use, although some plums can be stored successfully for short periods. The other fruits are usually made into preserves, or canned, frozen or dried for future use. Quinces can be stored if desired.

COLD STORAGE CELLAR

Unfortunately many people are not acquainted with or under-estimate the requisites of successful fruit storage. These requisites are based on the fact that the life processes of fruits after harvest are essentially chemical, and hence the rate at which they proceed (ripening) depends greatly upon temperature. *Apples freeze at about 28.5 degrees F. Hence it is necessary to keep them above this temperature.* A storage temperature of 32 degrees F. is usually maintained in commercial storages. Ripening and soft-ening of apples in storage is twice as rapid at 40 degrees F. as at 32 degrees F.; at 50 degrees it is almost double that at 40 de-grees, and at 70 degrees it is about twice as fast as at 50 degrees.

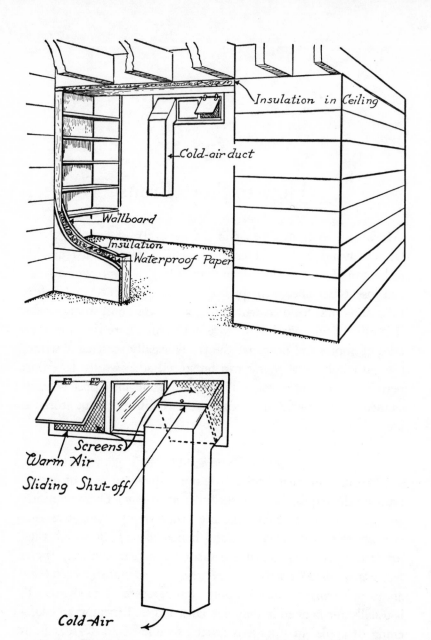

Insulation in Ceiling

Cold-air duct

Wallboard

Insulation

Waterproof Paper

Screens

Warm Air

Sliding Shut-off

Cold-Air

At top: Design for a cold storage room to be built in a cellar. Below: Detail of the ventilation arrangement. If this room is kept moist by sprinkling the floor or by other means, it will provide good storage for fruits and vegetables.

Therefore, for extended storage, prompt cooling of picked apples is essential, since they will ripen as much in one day at 70 degrees as they will in ten days at 30 degrees. For the home grower without refrigeration the recommended 32–34 degrees storage temperature is usually unattainable in the fall.

The best alternative is to keep the apples as cool as possible in unheated basements, or specially built, insulated fruit storage rooms. By regulating openings to the outside, advantage can be taken of the cooling effect of night air. In short, the room is ventilated when the outside air is cool, and kept closed when the air temperatures go up. Apples keep fairly well with temperatures as high as 40 degrees, but 35- to 40-degree temperatures are better. *The important point to remember is that for most successful storage, fruits must be kept cool.*

Keeping apples from wilting and shrivelling may be as important as keeping them from growing overripe, and can be done by maintaining a *relatively high humidity* in the storage. The higher the humidity in the air, the less the loss of moisture from stored fruits. Almost everyone realizes how dry the air is in heated rooms in winter. Under these conditions, water loss from fruits (which are about 85 per cent to 90 per cent water) is excessive, resulting in severe shrivelling and poor eating quality. Yet many apples are stored under such conditions! In suitable home storage, as, for example, a portion of a basement partitioned off and insulated and having access to the outside air, a favorable humidity can usually be maintained by occasionally wetting the floor with cool water. Often it is advantageous to sprinkle the walls, containers, and even the fruit itself. *In short, the humidity of the air surrounding the apples should be kept fairly high.*

Pears do not ripen as satisfactorily at cool storage temperatures as fall and winter apples. For highest eating quality, they should be taken out of storage while still fairly green and firm and ripened at room temperature. High humidity during ripening is very desirable. In the home, the use of wet cloths in and around a container is helpful. Some have suggested that pears keep better if wrapped in paper before storing.

Apples or other fruits should not be stored in close proximity to celery, cabbage or onions, because of the danger of taste contamination. Other vegetables, such as carrots, beets and pota-

A walk-in type of freezer, with a separate cooling chamber, is ideal for storing fruit. If a temperature close to freezing is maintained, apples will keep in condition for months.

toes, require somewhat similar storage conditions, and are often stored in the same room with apples quite satisfactorily. Packing apples and pears in clean, dry maple leaves seems to help not only in reducing moisture loss and consequent shrivelling but also in lessening absorption of odors from potatoes and other vegetables. Browning of the skin of apples in storage is often due to scald and can be prevented by wrapping each apple in a special oil-impregnated paper wrap.

Cherries, plums, peaches, nectarines and apricots must be dried, canned, or frozen for long storage.

Directions for canning, freezing and drying are readily available; hence, there is no need to go into details here.

13

Espaliers, a Fascinating Hobby

Although European fruit-growers have grown trellis-trained trees for many years, the practice has not been adopted to any great extent in this country. This has been due to our more extensive method of fruit growing and to unsatisfactory results of early trials with dwarf trees. Espalier fruit trees are suited to the hobbyist rather than the commercial fruit-grower. But for those who want something unique in fruit growing and who have the time and perseverance to give the attention required, the rigidly trained fruit tree offers decided possibilities. Set against walls, fences, trellises, trained on arbors, or used as hedges or specimen plants, trained dwarf fruit trees can be very successfully utilized. They are not, however, as suited to the average home orchard as the natural bush and little tree already described in detail.

A tree trained on a trellis is spoken of as an espalier. There are many variations in espalier training such as the single and multiple U-forms. Fans and palmettes are substantially central leader trees trained against walls. A cordon is started with the tree as a single, straight, unbranched stem. Its side branches are usually very much restricted and controlled with the result that they form mostly only short spurs.

Training is a mechanical process and is concerned with the placing of branches in definite, unnatural forms as they grow and develop. This is in contrast to the bush or little tree which requires relatively little specialized training since the natural form

A four-armed upright pear espalier in bloom, trained against a brick wall.

The espalier shown in the previous illustration, with pears ready to pick. This photo was taken the first year the espalier was set out in the location shown.

of growth is not altered to any great extent. As explained fully, earlier in the text, the usual practice with this type of dwarf tree training is to develop the main branches from an area well down on the main stem or trunk.

The pyramid tree is definitely a dominant leader type with radiating branches. Strong leader development is vital here. This type of training is well suited to upright-growing pear varieties. As an example of a complicated form, the winged pyramid requires more intensive training technique. Usually six arms are brought out at the base of the tree horizontally for 2 to 3 feet. Then they are bent upward and inward and are conducted along wires until they meet with the main stem of the tree 4 to 8 feet above. This requires much work and patience.

The espalier is usually trained on a wire trellis against a wall. In contrast to the three dimensional forms just described, espaliers really have only two dimensions—width and height. Many simple and complicated variations of espaliers are grown, including single, double, and triple U, and palmette verriers with variable numbers of arms. Fan espaliers are commonly used particularly in training peaches. Espalier training is often begun before the tree is a year old. Limbs (or arms) are tied to supports so that the desired forms can be attained. During the period of formative development which may require up to six years, careful attention to details of pruning and tying are required to develop and maintain each special form. This important early training is often done entirely by the nurseryman. The younger the trained tree is when purchased by the home-gardener the more attention must he give to formative training.

By training to a single stem, various cordons can be developed such as upright, oblique, horizontal, serpentine, etc. The single vertical or upright cordon is the simplest form, and can be tied to a single upright support. On the other hand, the double horizontal cordon requires two horizontal wires for the two sets of arms.

Delicious and Jonared apple espaliered on brick home.

BEST FORMS FOR THE DIFFERENT FRUITS

In the first place, the slower growing trees—pears and apples —are the better suited to the more elaborate forms of training. Dwarf pears succeed well as pyramids, cordons or espaliers. Dwarf apples are well suited for training to horizontal cordons and do well in various espalier arrangements. Pears and apples are also very easily grown as natural bushes or little trees as described earlier. The more free and rapid growing species such as the peach, nectarine, apricot, cherry, and Japanese plum are well-managed as fans, palmettes, or possibly as U's. The fan espalier form is very commonly and successfully grown. For dwarf prunes and plums the bush form is usually best. Quinces naturally grow as small trees or bushes but can be trained if desired.

EXTENT OF TRAINING IN THE NURSERY

It should be made perfectly clear that training is partly the job of the nurseryman and partly that of the home-gardener. A well-known nurseryman states that the average espalier offered for sale has been in training for a period of six years or more. Such trees require very little in the way of further formative training. The main requirement is form maintenance which is accomplished largely through pruning practices. If the home-gardener propagates his own trees, then training begins during the first or second year of growth in the nursery.

PRUNING ESPALIER AND OTHER TRAINED TREES

Naturally, the pruning of these highly trained trees requires much attention and very close observance to details and correct analysis of results. In order to keep the trees as perfectly balanced as possible and capable of producing maximum quantities of fruit, every branch, twig, and spur requires individual attention. Pinching back of vigorous-growing shoots, encouraging

A type of flexible plastic wrap is used by some orchardists to protect the trunk bark of small trees from the weather damage of extreme heat and cold, as well as from injury by gnawing rodents.

weak growths, bending down of branches to retard growth and promote fruit-bud formation are all in the pruning picture.

The pyramidal form, useful for pears, is developed from a whip headed back to 8 or 12 inches in height. The top bud develops the central leader. The other buds develop the laterals which are pinched back during the summer according to need. Dormant pruning each year consists of cutting back the leaders as required. A tree can be maintained at a specific height by the amount of dormant pruning back of the leaders. The lowest leaders should be longest and the average length of leaders should decrease as the top of the tree is approached. Summer pruning consists of pinching back side shoots on the leaders as required.

The palmette form is used to train trees on a trellis, wall or fence. The newly set untrained tree is pruned back severely. The top bud will form a new leader and two side buds on opposite sides of the main stem will develop into two lower arms. During the first summer, the other laterals from the main stem are usually pruned off to throw the vigor into the two main arms. The next season, two new oblique leaders or arms are developed above the lower ones. The small laterals are pinched back or pruned off as before. This process is repeated yearly until the desired number of arms has been attained. Each arm, of course, can be made to branch as much as desirable. The height and spread of a palmette can be adjusted and maintained by dormant heading back of leaders or arms.

In pruning vertical-branched espalier trees of apple, pear, plum and cherry, most side shoots should be kept cut back to about 4 inches by going over the trees once a month during July, August and September. The main leaders are pruned back in late winter or early spring, keeping the inner leaders about 6 inches shorter than the two end leaders. After the desired height is reached—from 5 to 12 feet—leaders are cut back to one eye, or bud, each year.

Cordons are branchless, spurred stems and can be trained vertically, obliquely or horizontally in single or double U- or V-shaped forms. The simplest form is upright and begins as a one-year tree cut back to 8 or 10 inches. Only one shoot is allowed to grow the first year with its lateral growths pinched back. Other shoots are pruned off. The dormant pruning consists of cutting back the leader at least 50 per cent to force spur-

V-Shaped Belgian Fence Individual Tree—Pear in Blossom.

ring, and pruning off all weak spurs and short branches. The other styles of cordons are similarly managed. The oblique and horizontal types must be trained to the correct position from the beginning, of course. With U- and V-shaped cordons, two leaders are required. With the U, the leaders are first trained horizontally for the desired distance and then vertically. With the horizontal cordon, side shoots are cut back to 6 inches. Since the fruit is borne on shoots that develop along the outer sides of the leader, only the shoots on the upper part of the leader are pruned off. The ends of the horizontal cordon are not pruned unless it is desired to prevent the tree from making new growth.

The fan form of espalier is started in the usual way by cutting back a one-year tree or by utilizing first-year branching if available. Selected shoots are allowed uninterrupted-length growth but the side shoots are pinched back. The desired shoots develop into the leaders. The subsequent summer pruning and dormant pruning is very important. With apple, pear, cherry and plum, all shoots developing along the leaders which form the tree framework are cut back to 8 to 10 inches once a month in July, August and September. Outward-growing side shoots are cut back to about 4 inches. The ends of the leaders are trimmed to control tree size. The completed fan may have eight to ten arms arranged in an orderly oblique fashion on the trellis.

Peach, nectarine and apricot trees trained to fans require dormant pruning-back of leaders to insure growth of side shoots. Some of these shoots are not pinched back but are allowed to become side shoots that will bear fruit. Since peaches and nectarines produce fruit only on the shoot growths of the previous summer, this development of side shoots is very important. In contrast to the apple, fruit spurs are not present and old wood is barren so far as fruiting is concerned. The shoots not saved for fruiting are pinched back during the summer months. A good method of insuring new fruiting wood is to pinch new shoots to two buds which will then develop into two new shoot growths. One of these is allowed to bloom and bear fruit the next season while the other is dormant-pruned to two buds to give the shoots for the following year.

The handling of the various espaliers is an art and not a science. No amount of description can substitute for actual experience. Two principal ideas, however, should always be kept in mind.

A 4-year-old pear espalier in blossom. This tree has grown so sturdily that supports are no longer needed.

First, it is the side shoots and not the leaders which need constant summer pruning. Pinching back these shoots induces the formation of fruit spurs, fruit buds and fruit. Second, leaders are the principal branches originating from the main trunk and are headed back, if necessary, usually in the dormant or winter season.

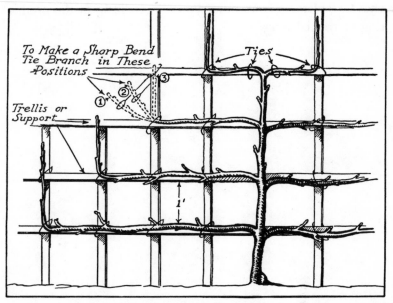

Training an espalier. Selected limbs are first carried out horizontally, then upright by means of ties to a supporting framework or fence.

METHODS OF FASTENING ESPALIER TREES

Stated very briefly, supports for wires must be sturdy and the wires should be taut at all times. The wires are placed or stretched where leaders or arms are, or will be, located. Leaders are tied to the wires with tarred twine or other suitably strong and weather-resistant cord. All ties should be made sufficiently loose to allow for growth and consequent increase in size of the leaders or arms.

Trellises of wooden laths can be used in place of wire supports if desired.

This discussion is intentionally brief since the main concern of this treatise is with the little tree or bush type of dwarf fruit tree—and not with the more complicated trained espaliers. Further information on the growing of these highly specialized types of dwarf fruit trees may be obtained from experienced growers or from nurserymen specializing in the production of trained trees.

Index